ALL THINGS

HAVE BECOME NEW,
WORK TOGETHER FOR GOOD,
ARE POSSIBLE

DANIEL T. NEWTON

© Copyright 2022 Daniel Newton, GP Publishing

www.graceplaceredding.com

Contributing authors and editors: Downing McDade, Katherine Marx, Eric Heinrichs, Daniel Fagot, Elizabeth Newton and the Grace Place Leadership Team

ISBN: 978-1-957601-02-1

"And we know that all things work together for good to those who love God, to those who are the called according to His purpose."

— Romans 8:28

Resources By Daniel Newton and Grace Place Ministries:

Truth in Tension: 55 Days to Living in Balance
Immeasurable: Reviewing the Goodness of God
Never Give Up: The Supernatural Power of Christlike Endurance
The Lost Art of Discipleship
The Lost Art of Discipleship Workbook
The Lost Art of Perseverance
All Things
GP Music: Beginnings – Worship Album

For more information on these books
and other inspiring resources, visit us at
www.GracePlaceMedia.com

Table of Contents

Foreword

Many years ago, while I was running around a track in a forested park near my home and enjoying a prayer time with the Lord, I noticed a majestic oak tree nearby. It was prominent amongst the other trees and boasted a large, strong, straight trunk and branches that hosted healthy and vibrant green leaves that glistened in the morning sun. There was a moderate wind blowing that morning, but the tree's trunk and branches were not moved in the slightest. As I admired this glorious creation, I prayed, "God, when I grow up and mature in You, I want to be just like that oak tree: strong, healthy, vibrant, and unwavering in the midst of the storms of life."

Many other trees of various species stood in the same forest as this oak. One of them was somewhat frail and had a bent trunk close to its foundation. As a result, it grew sideways and not straight. I remember thinking how sad it would be to grow crooked right from the very foundation of life. As I pondered this over the next couple of days, I again cried out to Him, "Lord, I want to grow straight!"

I wonder how many in the Body of Christ, because of inaccurate or incomplete teachings as new believers, have not grown to be straight, strong, and unwavering like that oak tree I admired that morning.

One of the things that has deeply grieved my heart through decades of serving the Body of Christ in ministry has been watching many believers struggle with their identity in Christ. I have concluded that, in most cases, the issue is rooted in a mindset based on outward religious performance that produces the fruit of striving, fear, insecurity, and an orphan-type of behavior. Without proper teaching and discipleship as new believers, we will fail to enjoy all the wonderful benefits of being new creations in Christ. God wants us to know that He has given Himself to us completely and has also given "all things that pertain to life and to godliness" (2 Peter 1:3 ESV). He has withheld nothing. It is all a gift because of His great love for us. There is nothing we need to work for or strive for. The fullness of every blessing in Christ is ours to discover and enjoy! What a wonderful Gospel! What a wonderful God!

True life in Christ is so different from the religious counterfeit that the enemy imposes on us. Daniel Newton's book, *All Things*, greatly refreshed me! It is a book that should be on every Christian's bookshelf, and every new believer would benefit significantly from understanding these truths. It is glorious to think of every new babe in Christ growing to be like the strong oak. You might be thinking, "But what about me? I think I've already grown up with a bent trunk." All things are possible in Christ, and He can realign you. He is not overwhelmed by anything and is not confined or limited in power. He will transform and free you from any mindsets that keep you from being all He has called you to be.

Foreward

This book will establish you on a journey of vital, foundational truth as you discover all the Lord has given you in Him! What has He given you? All Things! What has He done for you? All Things! Who is He to you? All Things!

"They will be called oaks of righteousness,
a planting of the Lord for the display of His splendor."
— Isaiah 61:3b (NIV)

Patricia King
Author, Minister, Media Producer and Host
patriciaking.com

Introduction

*"One of these days some simple soul will pick up the
Book of God, read it, and believe it. Then the rest of us
will be embarrassed."*
— Leonard Ravenhill

What do you see when you tell the story of your life?
For most of us, our stories are written in the confines of
logic-shaped boxes. Our hearts, minds, and beliefs can only
travel so far before hitting the invisible prison walls we've
built around us. We are defined by what we believe. More
importantly, we are defined by *who* we believe in.

Do you believe in a Savior that has the answer to life's most
difficult questions? Do you believe in a King who is triumphantly
leading you into victory every single day? Do you believe in a
God without limits?

That's our God. The One who created the heavens and the
earth. He is the Alpha and the Omega, the First and the Last. He
has no beginning, and He knows no end.

However, the world tells us a different story. When a
dream rises in your heart, it's natural to label it "impossible,"
"undoable," "illogical," or "foolish." Every limiting belief has a
gravity of its own, pulling you back toward "reality." You hear

people say, "Get your head out of the clouds!" or, "You're so heavenly-minded that you're no earthly good!"

We can't, however, condemn the people who say these things because it's *normal* to think that way. It was once *normal* to believe that the world is flat, that planets orbit the earth, or that running a mile in under four minutes is physically impossible. It was perfectly *normal* to believe these things—until someone proved otherwise. Then suddenly, the illogical became logical. Impossible became possible. Fantasy became reality.

We are called for this very thing: to stretch the limits, partake of His divine nature, and shake off the bondage of the *natural*. As believers, we are called to be a special, supernatural people (see 1 Peter 2:9), not a *natural* people. We are made in the image of the Almighty, destined to shape our reality through the manifestation of His holy presence.

What happens when we awaken to the reality of His limitless nature? What happens when we realize the Creator of life itself abides within us? Who or what could possibly stop us?

When you realize God has no limits, life takes on a whole new meaning. Every day becomes a coloring book with no lines. There are no limits to who you can be in Christ and what you can do. Why? Because our Heavenly Father is not the God of *some* things. He's the God of *all* things.

What do you believe? Do you feel stuck, limited, or even apathetic toward this journey known as life? Does waking up feel like stepping into a neverending hamster wheel, spinning and spinning, but going nowhere? Do you feel bound by your past, absent in the present, or fearful of the future?

Well, there's good news.

Introduction

The God of *all* things is madly in love with you. He is working on your behalf, aligning the impossible puzzle pieces of your life into perfect order. He can and will make all things new. He turns even the worst situations around for good so that all things become possible for you.

> *"He who did not spare His own Son, but delivered Him up for us all, how shall He not with Him also freely give us all things?"*
> — *Romans 8:32*

You're going to be reading that phrase throughout the pages to come: *All Things*. My hope is that your mind would be washed with the water of the Word over and over as you are continually renewed by His truth. As Psalm 18:19 says, "He also brought me out into a broad place; He delivered me because He delighted in me." God desires to bring you into a spacious place, into open pastures where not even the sky is the limit! He wants to deliver you from the miry clay of life to set you high above the natural patterns of this world. In Christ, our horizon stretches into eternity, our discovery is unending, and our joy is without measure.

The phrase "all things" is repeated throughout the Word of God, emphasizing the totality of what Jesus accomplished for us. The blood of Jesus and the working power of His redemption have no limitations. Because of this, there are no borderlines to what God can do in and through your life! In Jesus, God made provision for all things, and it is now our privilege to access, receive, and experience everything He paid for.

This revelation has truly changed my life. In 2006, I did a Bible study to seek out everything Jesus did on our behalf. I saw it repeatedly in the scriptures that His life, death, and resurrection unlocked an inheritance that all of His children can freely walk in. This passage especially stood out to me as a clear definition of His divine exchange:

> *"Surely He has borne our griefs and carried our sorrows; yet we esteemed Him stricken, smitten by God, and afflicted. But He was wounded for our transgressions, He was bruised for our iniquities; the chastisement for our peace was upon Him, and by His stripes we are healed. All we like sheep have gone astray; we have turned, every one, to his own way; and the Lord has laid on Him the iniquity of us all."*
> *— Isaiah 53:4-6*

Jesus suffered so we could reign in life. He paid the necessary price for us to walk in freedom. He took our sin, our poverty, our sickness, our depression, our anxiety, and every other disempowering issue we could ever face and buried them in His grave. Three days later, He rose again with not even a speck of our old nature attached to Him. Our limited, sinful, law-bound nature was killed and abandoned once and for all.

> *"For the love of Christ compels us, because we judge thus: that if One died for all, then all died..."*
> *— 2 Corinthians 5:14*

Jesus has done it all. His victory is your own! When you realize the power of grace, you open yourself up to an overflow of His kindness. Everything pertaining to life and godliness is available for those who have said yes to His perfect blood and received His full package of salvation. When you realize it's *all* because of Him, you can thrive in *all* areas of your life!

As I've studied the Word and the victory of the Cross, I have found three life-changing truths about God's character that I want to share with you.

1. HE MAKES *ALL THINGS* NEW
"Behold, I am making all things new" (Rev. 21:5).

2. HE WORKS *ALL THINGS* TOGETHER FOR GOOD
"And we know that all things work together for good to those who love God, to those who are the called according to His purpose" (Rom. 8:28).

3. HE MAKES *ALL THINGS* POSSIBLE
"With men this is impossible, but with God all things are possible" (Matt. 19:26).

I realized how clear it was that He is the God of *all* things! He doesn't go halfway—He's all in! God doesn't ration Himself out to us like a military general reluctantly sending reinforcements on the battlefield. He is backing us with the full force of heaven's armies! When Jesus died on the Cross, His blood paved a way for us to enter the fullness of His presence. We have access to *all* He is, and it's *all* by grace!

My good deeds cannot make anything new, but by being co-crucified and co-resurrected with Christ, I come into union with His Spirit, and my old earthly nature passes away. All things work together for good, not because of *my* efforts to right my own wrongs, but because He accomplished the ultimate good on the Cross. All things are possible, not because of *my* strength or ability, but because of Him and what He has accomplished—His finished work. The Word does not say, "I can do all things." It says, "I can do all things *through Christ who strengthens me*" (Phil. 4:13). For too long we have made the Gospel about us when it has been about Him all along.

These revelations radically shifted my focus. It took me from self-consciousness to Christ-consciousness and from the law to grace. I understand that nothing is about me; it's *all* about Him. Everything that happens in my life is because of Jesus and what

He did. Now I daily recognize His favor, grace, and blessing on my life, and I know I haven't strived for them. They come from Him, and knowing this positions me to receive even more of what He's done. On a weekly basis, people tell me how favored I am because of the breakthroughs and miracles I see and the great resolutions that come from negative circumstances. I tell them that it's not my favor but Christ's, and I'm just walking in the favor He already paid for each of us to have.

I believe that as you read this book, you too will start to see that everything is about Jesus. As you do, the words in Matthew 6:33 will come alive: "Seek first the kingdom of God and His righteousness, and *all these things* shall be added to you" (emphasis added). As you focus on Him, He will make all things new, all things work together for good, and all things possible by His grace.

Part One

ALL THINGS HAVE BECOME NEW

*"Do not remember the former things, nor consider the
things of old. Behold, I will do a new thing, now it
shall spring forth; shall you not know it? I will even
make a road in the wilderness
and rivers in the desert."*

— Isaiah 43:18-19

Chapter One

All, Not Some

"...I make all things new..."
— Revelation 21:5

What do you think when you hear the phrase, "all things"? How far can your imagination run before you come face-to-face with your limitations? How exhaustive is your definition of "all"? How often does the voice of what's practical, logical, and "normal" hush the voice of the supernatural? Many of our hearts have been taught by the world to look no further, think no higher, and believe no greater than what's right in front of us.

It's easy to write off "all" as "some," especially when we hear a phrase like the verse above: "all things new."

Really? Are *all* things new?

How could all things be made new? I know what I've done. I know the kind of person I've been. I know the pain, hurt, and regret I'm going through.

In light of these questions, feelings, and emotions, we need to understand what actually happened when Jesus came to the earth. What's the cause and effect of a spotless Lamb being crucified on our behalf? Does the blood of Jesus really cover *all* of our sins? It's easy to sprinkle it here and there on certain areas of our lives but equally as easy to omit from others because we can't comprehend the possibility of "all."

We can look at the parts of our lives where God is already working and believe that all things have become new in those places, but what about everywhere else? What about the circumstances that look the same as they did before you were born again? Can you believe that all things have become new in *those* places, and not just the ones already manifesting redemption?

What do we do with those "stuck" situations that feel unredeemed and untouched by forgiveness? We are born again but still drowning in debt, struggling with an addiction, suffering from a chronic disease, or having family problems.

If all things are new, what do we do with the areas that we are still waiting to see God's goodness? Does our lack of experience make the Bible less true? Does it mean the Word of God is false? Have we done something wrong to limit the power of God working in our lives? How do we explain this?

These are real thoughts we can all grapple with. Sometimes it feels as though there's a thick, invisible line between what's been promised and what's actually happening. When God told Abraham he would be the father of many nations, he and his wife were old and barren! How could something new and alive come from something dead? It's because of this very important key—God gives life to the dead and calls those things which do not exist as though they did (see Rom. 4:17).

He is the God of all things. He is the God of the impossible. When Jesus came to make you new, He did a complete work.

(To learn more about the finished work of the Cross, see my book, *It Is Finished*.) You aren't partially new. You are fully new!

The Good News is Actually Good

The word "all" comes from the Greek word *pas*. And guess what? It truly does mean *all*—not some or most, but "each, any, all, the whole." It's not an exaggeration to say "all things are being made new"—it's scriptural. When God said, "I make all things new," He revealed His plan for humanity. He revealed His nature as a redeemer. Ever since sin entered the world, all of us have needed God's redeeming power. We've all made mistakes both big and small. None of us have a perfect track record. We all have areas of our lives that could use an upgrade!

This promise of newness is not something reserved for those who have died and gone to heaven. For all who come to Him, God promises to give new life. God's will is for the newness of His heavenly realities to invade the earth. Our brand new life in Christ is for the here and now because "[He] is the same yesterday, today, and forever" (Heb. 13:8).

That's the reality of the Gospel! It's the "Good News" of Jesus Christ. In order for it to be good news, it must actually be *good*. If the Gospel seems to work in some areas of our lives but not in all things, then we need to take the limits off our perception of who God is toward us. Don't just settle for what you *think* can be made new. Believe God wants *all things* made new.

> *"[God] raised us up together, and made us sit together in the heavenly places in Christ Jesus, that in the ages to come He might show the exceeding riches of His grace in His kindness toward us in Christ Jesus."*
>
> — *Ephesians 2:6-7*

The tangible power, goodness, and mercy of God have been released in the message of the Gospel. Read the passage above again. God raised you up in order to show the world the riches of His grace through His kindness toward you. Now that's good news! God raised you from the old, dead, sinful nature of your past as a declaration to the world of how good He is. He made you new, not because you're good, but because He is!

It's this good news that carries the very power to transform us. As Paul writes, "For I am not ashamed of the Gospel, because it is the power of God that brings salvation to everyone who believes..." (Rom. 1:16 NIV). The Gospel contains the potential, power, and ability to save us and redeem every aspect of our lives. When we believe in the goodness of His nature, we walk in union with our perfect and holy Father.

If you see areas of your life that are not lining up with the Gospel, take heart and do not be discouraged. Receiving His newness comes by grace, which is released when we believe in the goodness of God. We are all being perfected through the power of His unmerited lovingkindness. None of us have attained perfection, but we're called to it. However, it can only be done by grace which comes through believing who He is: "Grace and peace be multiplied to you in the knowledge of God and of Jesus our Lord" (2 Peter 1:2). If there is an area of your life that isn't reflecting His goodness yet, don't worry. Just keep receiving from Him. Keep believing He is good even when it feels, looks, and seems like nothing else is.

Sozo

One of the most iconic verses in the Bible is John 3:16: "For God so loved the world that He gave His only begotten Son, that whoever believes in Him should not perish but have everlasting life." This is amazing news and an incredible truth, but did you know there's a greater meaning to Jesus' message? The importance of this scripture comes to light in the verse that follows: "For God did not send His Son into the world to condemn the world, but that the world through Him might be saved" (John 3:17).

The word translated as "saved" in this verse is the Greek word *sozo*. *Sozo* is a powerful word, and to define it simply as "saved" undermines what God wants to do in our lives.

In the original Greek, *sozo* can also be translated as "cured, preserved, set free, healed, rescued from danger, kept safe, restored, made whole, and made prosperous." When God "saved" us, this was not just a ticket to heaven or a "get-out-of-jail-free" card. He rescued us from darkness, delivered us into the Kingdom of light, healed us completely, made us whole, and much more. There is no detail of your life that God's salvation has overlooked! Every benefit you can imagine has been paid for; it's your belief that will either block or bring forth these blessings.

The Original Point of Opportunity

Let's take a closer look at the concept of redemption. Jesus provided unmerited grace to humanity through the Cross. We are fully redeemed by the blood of Jesus, and we are no longer held back by the mistakes of our past. To "redeem" means to restore back to the original point of opportunity. There is no barrier between us and God that He has not overcome through the sacrifice of Jesus. We are forgiven of all our sins, so every connection we have to our past mistakes is severed forever!

What is the original point of opportunity? When we received Christ into our lives, He did *more* than simply clean the slate. God didn't just put us back to neutral. If that's all that happened, we would be left to our own devices to "self-sustain" our salvation from here on out. The Good News would only be half-good. Yes, our sins would be blotted out, but what about tomorrow? We think, *What if I make a mistake again? What if I can't measure up?* If this was all salvation was, then we would resort to biting our lips, clenching our fists, and performing for holiness. We would live under the weight of the past and in the tormenting fear of future failures. However, Jesus died to set us free from our sin (past, present, and future) *and* its effects on our lives.

God now looks at us as if we had never sinned in the first place! We were returned to the original point of opportunity, just like Adam before he had eaten the fruit in the Garden of Eden. It's a brand new start with a brand new nature. We get to live a life free from the grip of sin and its destruction, perfectly at peace with God. We are fully free to live without the fear of judgment because our sins have been judged and atoned for through the Cross of Jesus Christ. We are free from anything that would hinder us from union with God. "All" means "all." Jesus' sacrifice has fully redeemed us, bringing us into perfect, uninterrupted fellowship with Him.

"For I will be merciful to their unrighteousness, and their sins and their lawless deeds I will remember no more."
— Hebrews 8:12

You Can't Fix This

You might be thinking, *This sounds great and all, but I got myself into this mess, so I have to get myself out.* That may sound noble, but that's not the Gospel. Romans 5:17 says, "For if by the one man's (Adam's) offense death reigned through the one, much more those who receive abundance of grace and of the gift of righteousness will reign in life through the One, Jesus Christ."

So, through Adam's offense, death reigned. This means the destruction you experienced before you accepted Jesus didn't start with you. You were paying the price for the debt of sin traced all the way back to Adam. Every one of us was born into a sinful nature through the transgression of Adam—we were born into sin! However, as the verse goes on to say, we will reign in life when we receive the abundance of grace and the gift of righteousness given by another Man, Jesus Christ.

We were given salvation we couldn't earn to blot out a problem that didn't start with us and that we were powerless to change. Where in this equation is there an option for someone to "get themselves out"? There is none—it's impossible! Humanity could never cure the plague of sin and death that it started. We needed someone else to rescue us. This is why Jesus came! We could *never* reverse, change, or make up for the sins of mankind.

God's Hand of Redemption

I mentor many young adults in my ministry, Grace Place (see the back of this book for more information about Grace Place Ministries). For a time, we sent teams out regularly to minister in the local community and pray for people on the streets. Over the years, we have seen God do some amazing things in many people.

One particular day, two of our students approached a homeless man holding a cardboard sign in a store parking lot. He had a brace on his right hand, so when they went to shake hands, he had to shake with his left hand. They learned he had just gotten out of the hospital from breaking his hand in three places. A week prior, he had punched a tree with his bare hand after discovering that his girlfriend had cheated on him. He had struggled most of his life with anger, so when he found out she had cheated on him, he lashed out and seriously hurt himself.

The two students prayed for him to be healed and then asked him to try doing something he hadn't done before to test his injury. He took off his brace, started moving his wrist around, and was shocked to find that his pain level had decreased dramatically. He was able to crack his knuckles and squeeze his hand into a fist, both of which he hadn't been able to do since breaking it. They prayed for him again, and afterward his pain was completely gone and he had full mobility back in his hand! When they left, he even shook hands with them using his right hand, and the brace he had been wearing was tossed on the ground behind him.

God never ties us to our past mistakes. He sometimes even sets us free from the consequences of our own bad choices. Yes, there may be times where we need to reconcile with people we've hurt, but God is not waiting to pour His wrath out on us. He has forgiven us. He doesn't want us to regard ourselves according to those things anymore. "As far as the east is from the west, so far He has removed our transgressions from us" (Psalm 103:12). If we always dwell on what we've done wrong, then we will miss how He has made us right!

Just think again about how scandalous this man's testimony is. The man punched a tree so hard that he broke his own hand. Then, a couple of believers show up in his life, and suddenly, he's healed! The supernatural forgiveness of God was manifested in that moment. The guy clearly "deserved" to have a broken hand—he punched a tree! Yet God, in His mercy, made it as though the man had never retaliated in a rage. The work of Jesus is so complete and so far-reaching!

Jesus died to accomplish what we could not. Even if you've brought something upon yourself, redemption always runs deeper. Think about this: Adam *deliberately* disobeyed God when he ate the forbidden fruit. Jesus came to free us from the power of the curse that was put on us. Through His eternal redemption, we no longer have to experience the ramifications of Adam's sin or our past mistakes. Again, He not only removed your sins but the effects of those sins as well!

A New Covenant

When Jesus died, the veil that once stood between mankind and the presence of God was torn from top to bottom. This was no happenstance; the veil was six inches thick. No man could possibly tear the veil in his own strength. It had to be God. And with this act, He was forever saying, "There is no separation between you and Me. The way is open for you to enter into the Holy of Holies. The Law and all its requirements have been fulfilled!" Jesus set us free from the Old Covenant that man could not keep. He freed us from the law!

When I say "the law," I'm not merely referring to the Mosaic Law or to the complex system of ordinances and sacrifices that allowed Israel to live in the presence of a Holy God. While these are included in the law, I am referring to something broader. It is the system of thinking that tells us to perform for love, work for acceptance, and fight for a sense of worth. Many people think they're not living under the law. While that is scripturally true, they are still living in bondage to it. If you find yourself constantly measuring the weight of your actions and behavior to earn a good relationship with God, you're still caught in a cycle of religious performance.

Deeply ingrained into the nature of humanity is this simple yet profound truth: When wrong is committed, someone has to make up for it. A price needs to be paid. It wouldn't be fair otherwise. So, for thousands of years, mankind has done one of two things when he's committed sin: ignored it or did what he could to make up for it.

The temple system established in Israel was the best option for humanity to atone for their sins at the time. "Indeed, under the law almost everything is purified with blood, and without the shedding of blood there is no forgiveness of sins" (Heb. 9:22 ESV). The religious structure ran in this way: if you sin, there must be blood—there must be an offering. However, it was never enough. The blood of bulls and goats could never wash the deepest places of their hearts. It could only temporarily lift the consequence of having fallen short. There was a need for a better sacrifice—an eternal one!

Since we were little, the law has indoctrinated us with this "temple-system" pattern of thinking. The temple was the way Israel related to God: "We bring a sacrifice, He forgives us of our sins." It's this very mindset that has leaked into the way we think and live in the present. However, we must realize that Jesus came, not with the blood of a bull or a goat, but with His own blood! He became the sacrifice, once and for all. Jesus is the atonement for the sins of the whole world. Just as John the Baptist declared, "Behold! The Lamb of God who takes away the sin of the world!" (John 1:29).

"...[He] loved us and washed us from our sins in His own blood."
— Revelation 1:5

The law's influence on us today is a web of mindsets that say, "You must *do* this to *get* that." "You haven't done enough." "You missed the mark there." When you live with a law-based mindset, you will feel as if you deserve punishment for your mistakes even though Christ already took the punishment for you. You feel that there is always another sacrifice to be made, always another offering to give, and always another "act of holiness" to justify your shortcomings. It's plain to see that the system of the law, with its strict commandments, is not the Gospel! Jesus' laid down life, perfect unconditional love, and selfless sacrifice—*that's* the Gospel!

"...by Him everyone who believes is justified from all things from which you could not be justified by the law of Moses."
— Acts 13:39

Did you see that? Through Christ, God has set you free from all things that the law never could! Jesus took care of all your works that hindered you from justification and all the sins you couldn't atone for! Now, all you have to do is believe that *He* is the sacrifice for *all* of your mistakes. You could *never* settle the case for your sins. Your own works, confessions, and good deeds will never be enough to justify you. *He* is the offering, *He* is the atonement, and *He* is your perfection! His sacrifice isn't just enough for *some* of your faults but is sufficient for *all* of your imperfect thoughts, feelings, and actions.

"Your Sins are Forgiven"

Matthew 9 and Luke 5 record a powerful healing meeting Jesus carried out in someone's home. Many people were receiving miracles and hearing the Good News of the Kingdom. In the midst of this, a group of men climbed onto the roof, cut a hole in the ceiling, and lowered down their paralyzed friend on a mat right in front of Jesus. In response to the incredible amount of faith the men showed in Jesus, He said to the paralyzed man, "Son, be of good cheer; your sins are forgiven you" (Matt. 9:2). It's interesting to note that the man didn't come with the mindset of getting his sins forgiven. He came to be healed. However, by forgiving this man, Jesus was revealing a greater truth.

Also present in the house were the Pharisees, a group of religious teachers. When they heard Jesus' statement to the paralyzed man, they were offended because they perceived that Jesus was doing something that only God could do: forgive sins. Jesus knew their thoughts and decided to take the scene a step further. He said, "Which is easier, to say, 'Your sins are forgiven you,' or to say, 'Arise and walk'?" Jesus linked the forgiveness of sins to physical healing. Which was the greater miracle? The healing or the forgiveness of his sins? The truth is that they are both parts of the same miracle of salvation.

Healing is a natural byproduct of the forgiveness of God. Forgiveness of sin opens the door for healing, and healing points back to His forgiveness. Jesus' interaction with the paralyzed man would have been incomplete if He had simply forgiven his sins and not healed him. This is salvation in its completion, and it applies to every area of life. Those who experience the full *sozo* package in Christ are able to walk in complete healing, not just the forgiveness of sins.

Jesus wants us to exchange our "old" for His "new." Anywhere there seems to be a restriction or limitation, there is provision for newness in the blood of Jesus. We must see Jesus get everything He paid for by allowing the finished work of the Cross to have its full effect.

He Is Willing

God paid the ultimate price to save us. We often think of sickness and disease as large obstacles. We marvel at miraculous stories in Scripture, such as the multiplication of the loaves and fish or the splitting of the Red Sea. However, a far greater miracle is when someone is born again into a new nature through the blood of Jesus. This miracle of salvation is what cost Jesus His own life. He freely gave His life so we could be saved! And if He "did not spare His own Son, but delivered Him up for us all, how shall He not with Him also freely give us all things?" (Rom. 8:32).

Why would God hold anything back from us if He's already given His Son? Why would Jesus, who willingly laid down His life, suddenly change His mind and hold back good things from us once we have been saved? He wouldn't. Luke 5 also records the story of a leper coming to Jesus. In fear and trembling, he fell at Jesus' feet and said, "Lord, if You are willing, You can make me clean." Jesus' reply was simple and yet profound: "I am willing."

Throughout His entire ministry, people would come to Jesus needing healing and breakthrough, and every time, He met them and displayed the same heart: "I am willing." They got the breakthrough every time. They received healing every time. They found redemption every time. This is the character of

Jesus Christ. We have access to everything we need—we only need to receive it.

Expect Newness

Many of us are not *experiencing* newness because we are not *expecting* newness. Often the Church teaches that we are saved by grace. However, are we teaching that salvation extends to each area of our lives by this same grace? How will we walk in the fullness of salvation if we are not taught to expect that all things will become new when we are saved? Instead of holding ourselves back by what we have been taught or our beliefs about ourselves, we must have faith in what the Word of God says. Receiving from God requires the complete surrender of our doubts and fears and the willingness to believe in His promises, even if we don't yet see evidence of their fulfillment.

We must never allow ourselves to lower our beliefs to match our experiences. We will never experience more if we do not dare to believe God for more. If our experiences do not support or match what Scripture says is true, we must choose to trust that God will always come through. If we do not let God define our experience, our experience will become our god.

Faith Sees Beyond

Hebrews 11:1 says that "faith is...the evidence of things *not seen*." John 1:18 (NIV) says that "no one has ever seen God," meaning that God exists in a realm that can only be accessed by faith. To encounter Him, we must move beyond what we can experience with our five senses. Like Peter, we must step out of the boat and into the impossible. When God created the world, He spoke to *nothing* and created *something*. His nature is to speak to that which does not exist and create something beyond our expectations.

If you're not experiencing the fullness of salvation, don't allow yourself to be discouraged. Don't allow yourself to focus on what *isn't* happening. This only creates more faith in your "limitations" and undermines your faith in God! Raise your expectations to match your beliefs. Put your focus on what God has said and refuse to budge from there. Plant your flag in that place and build a house there. God's Word will never return to Him void without accomplishing His purpose (see Is. 55:11). Choose to believe that all things are made new, even if you have yet to see it. The simple truth is that if you want to see it, you must first trust Him.

Is there an area of your life that is being restricted? Ask God to wash your mind with the nature of who He is in that area. Every limitation is the result of a limiting belief, not just about yourself, but about God's goodness toward you. His love for you is so unlimited that, if you would only tap into a fraction of its power, your life would never be the same!

Every wall you've built around your heart is ready to come tumbling down. Every voice that says, "You can't be made new in *this* area" is about to be silenced. Why? Because God came in the likeness of human flesh to break your limits, demolish your sins, and conquer your fears. God wants to renew your mind so you can see the entirety of what He's done for you. He wants to unlock your full potential, and this comes through understanding that you are completely new despite what you have experienced in the past. The more you see Him as the perfect offering for *all* of your sins, the more you will realize, "Wow, I really am new!"

> *"But when Christ had offered for all time a single sacrifice for sins, he sat down at the right hand of God, waiting from that time until his enemies should be made a footstool for his feet. For by a single offering he has perfected for all time those who are being sanctified."*
>
> *— Hebrews 10:12-14 (ESV)*

Chapter Two

The Old is Gone

"As far as the east is from the west,
so far has He removed our transgressions from us."
— Psalm 103:12

"What is your name?" Jesus asked. The man fell on his knees before Him. A demonic stronghold had so violently gripped him that he hardly resembled the man he used to be. Nobody knew him by his real name anymore. They only knew him by what they saw and heard—his screams, terror, and oppressive acts of violence and anger. They knew him by his insanity, his brokenness.

When he spoke to Jesus, it was not with the voice of a single man, but a multitude of demons. "My name is Legion, for we are many." This was not the name of a man but of a military operation. In Roman rule, a legion of troops consisted of about five thousand men. Regardless of how many demons had taken up residence inside him, it was apparent to Jesus that the man was completely overtaken. This man was a prisoner of war held hostage within his own body, and for years he had been forced to obey the bidding of his demonic masters. However, everything was about to change.

When Jesus stepped foot on the shore of the Gadarenes, a superior Kingdom arrived with Him. In a moment, His dominion was established. The King of all creation had come, and compared to His authority, the foreboding armies of darkness had no chance.

Suddenly, in coming face-to-face with his Creator, the man was alone in his own mind and in control of his own body. In a single moment, all the long years of torment and oppression were washed away, never to return. Whatever labels society had given him to explain his condition were now irrelevant. He had become an entirely new person with an entirely new destiny.

This man went on to spread the Good News of Jesus Christ to his entire region. He begged to follow Jesus, who had completely redefined his reality, identity, and potential. However, Jesus, knowing the power of what had taken place, sent the man back to his town to proclaim the truth of God's Kingdom. He was not simply freed from the past—he was set up for a glorious future because all things had become new. His story was no longer shameful but an incredible testimony to the limitless reach of the love and power of God. The old was gone, and the new had come.

This story is told in three of the gospels (Matthew 8, Mark 5, and Luke 8). What amazes me the most is the sharp contrast between the deep darkness this man had fallen into and the passionate seeker of Christ he suddenly became. For years his identity was buried beneath the weight of constant demonic torment. Yet it only took a moment for the King of Kings to overturn the pain he had grown so accustomed to. Yes, Jesus makes all things new! When He steps foot on the shore of your heart, any residue of darkness, pain, and brokenness must bow before Him. Problems tremble in the presence of His supreme authority and holy majesty.

This man's instantaneous transformation could never have happened in his own strength. He could have spent the rest of his life alone in that graveyard without a fraction of change taking place. The miracle rested entirely upon the shoulders of Jesus Christ. It was *His* qualification, *His* unending love, and *His* unmerited grace that overwhelmed the tormenting forces of darkness. With Jesus, our entire reality can completely change in a moment because where light is, darkness cannot exist. His life conquers any remnant of death abiding within us, no matter how dark, scary, or lonely it may seem.

He Died for ALL of You

When Jesus died for you, He didn't die for the "good parts" of you. He died for *all* of you. The sinful, broken, wicked nature of your humanity was permanently thrown into the sea of forgetfulness. Your past, with your mistakes and failures, was washed away. When you gave Jesus your life, He made you into an entirely new creation. "Therefore, if anyone is in Christ, he is a new creation; old things have passed away; behold, all things have become new" (2 Cor. 5:17). The old man that enslaved us to his will has died, and we are now alive in Christ.

This isn't just a lesson we read about in an ancient book. It's an ever-present reality. Jesus doesn't come, fix you up, and then leave you on your own. He makes your heart a home and constantly sustains your identity as a new creation. We aren't inviting Jesus in to stay the night—He comes to abide forever! He wants access to every room in your heart! He wants to fill *all* you are with His light, life, and love!

Neos vs. Kainos

Being born again is not a restoration back to a previous state. It is not simply undoing the bad things we've done or that have been done to us. We become something completely new, something that has not existed before. It's not like buying a brand new pair of shoes—it's like buying a brand new pair of *flying shoes*! They have never been seen before and are completely different in nature than last year's ordinary sneakers! When we surrendered our lives to Jesus, we did not become refurbished versions of our former selves. We became new in every way.

The word "new" in 2 Corinthians 5:17 comes from the Greek word *kainos*, meaning, "of a new kind, unprecedented, unheard of before." You aren't an updated version of what you once were. You are something the world has never seen before! This is possible because of the nature of Christ's sacrifice. Jesus did not just die *for* you—He died *as* you. When Jesus died, you died. Galatians 2:20 says, "I have been crucified with Christ; *it is no longer I who live*, but Christ lives in me; and the life which I now live in the flesh I live by faith in the Son of God, who loved me and gave Himself for me" (emphasis added).

Jesus did not put a bandage over your sinful nature. He took it onto the Cross and killed it. When He was resurrected, you were resurrected with Him into newness of life (Rom. 6:4). However, you were not raised as you were before, back into your old man, chained to the desires of sin and death. You were born again as a spotless and unblemished being, holy and blameless before the Lord. When we entered into relationship with Jesus, our old kingdom of self was put to death along with its sinful nature. We were co-crucified with Christ. Not only that, but we were also co-buried with Christ, solidifying the end of sin's reign over us.

What is the best part? We were not left in the grave. Just like Jesus, we were raised to life! We are co-resurrected with Christ and given new life through Him! We died, and our lives are now hidden with Christ in God (see Col. 3:3). We are brought back to life to experience it "on earth as it is in heaven," regardless of what we have been through (see Matt. 6:10). All things have been made new!

Jesus Defines Us

John 1:3 says, "All things were made through Him, and without Him nothing was made that was made." Jesus has intimate, inside knowledge about all of creation and, more importantly, our lives. This means that we do not define reality as we see fit. That privilege belongs to Him and Him alone. This is an important distinction because it means that when Jesus says something is true about us, it is true about us for all time.

It doesn't matter what our experiences have been, how many good or bad things have happened to us, or all the right and wrong we have done. We are still defined by Jesus. Despite our feelings of qualification or disqualification, or what other people have called us or said about us, Jesus is the only person with the power to give us an identity. He says, "You are a new creation." That is the truth regardless of what our experiences tell us.

Too many Christians are living theoretically "new" lives but still seeing themselves according to their old pattern of existence. They limit their beliefs about their potential in light of what they've experienced, failing to take hold of their new identity in Christ. Holding onto condemnation from past mistakes, they assume that because they haven't forgiven themselves, God hasn't either. These beliefs hold them back from living in the newness they have every right and ability to claim! Choosing to believe lies instead of the truth of God puts faith in the enemy's influence in our lives. We end up living under the very limitations we expect.

Imagine if the man of the Gadarenes had this limited mindset. He went from the notorious reject of the town to the notorious evangelist. According to the standard held by many believers today, this man had a "valid" excuse to reject his new identity. He could have focused on his past and been filled with shame for the monster he had become. *Who am I to think God could use me?* After all, he was pretty "unworthy" of doing great things for God. Thank God he didn't think like this!

Instead, he no longer identified with his past. He was so transformed that his reputation was completely restored. His past was not a limitation on his future. He spread the news about Jesus throughout his entire region, without feelings of disqualification or shame, because he knew that he had been made an entirely new man. He hadn't attempted to change his life by simply improving his habits or trying harder. God displayed His mercy to him and completely set him free. This man could testify of what Jesus had done because he knew he would never be the same again.

Jesus wants to do a new thing in *your* life! God the Father wants us to experience freedom so much that He sent His only Son to die and wash our past away. Now that we are in Christ, we must identify with Him, letting the old things go. Take God's encouragement from Isaiah 43:18-19: "Do not remember the former things, nor consider the things of old. Behold, I will do a new thing, now it shall spring forth; shall you not know it?..."

No Condemnation

"There is therefore now no condemnation to those who are in Christ Jesus."
— Romans 8:1

Jesus' work on the Cross did not only set you free from the consequences of your past sin. He set you free into a new life. He accomplished everything so that you don't have to live under the weight of what you've failed to do, nor the weight of what you have yet to do. You can be free from the negative effects of condemnation!

When a building is condemned, what does that mean? It means the government is declaring that the structure is no longer fit to be lived in. It's useless, dilapidated, and destined for destruction. In fact, the building actually devalues the property it's built on. It would be better if it weren't there at all! Nobody would come and live in that house because it would be dangerous and uninhabitable!

Think further with me. The Bible calls us the temples of the Holy Spirit (see 1 Cor. 6:19). We are the house of God! When you met Jesus, He came and He knocked on the door of your heart. What does that say about you? You must not be a condemned house. No matter how much you might feel that way, no one is condemning you. God hasn't hung a warning sign on the door of your life saying "DO NOT ENTER." In fact, He purchased your house altogether, ripped off the old signage, and built an entirely new structure. The King of Kings wants to come and live in you. When Jesus comes, He considers you fit to be lived in! He qualifies you as a perfect dwelling place for His holy presence. So when we give in to condemnation, we are essentially saying, "Because of my actions, I am unfit for the

Spirit to live in me." However, what's the truth? Jesus is standing at the door! He wants to come in and commune with you!

> *"Behold, I stand at the door and knock. If anyone hears My voice and opens the door, I will come in to him and dine with him, and he with Me."*
> — *Revelation 3:20*

Condemnation is one of the believer's greatest obstacles. It is the enemy's strategy to halt our effectiveness today by distracting us with what we have done in the past. He wants us distracted by the false reality of yesterday—a "reality" where Christ's work wasn't enough to redeem us. Condemnation tells us Christ's work in us was ineffective. *It may work for other people but not for you or me.* It convinces us we are our biggest enemy and traps us in a cycle of self-effort and self-focus where we have to prove we are not the people we used to be. This is why the truth that we are saved "by grace... and that not of [our] selves" is so powerful (Eph. 2:8).

The Gospel completely sets us free from yesterday's mistakes. Even if the world points a finger at us and says, "You're still the same old person you used to be," the truth is, our old man is dead in Christ. We must "stand fast therefore in the liberty by which Christ has made us free, and...not be entangled again with a yoke of bondage," which is the law (Gal. 5:1). Jesus has made all things new in your life, and walking in this reality comes by first forgetting the past. We cannot remain tied to what we've done or failed to do! If we set our minds on our past, we will be bombarded with the guilt of yesterday along with all of its negative side effects. All things truly are new. We can have hope for every single area of our lives because we are no longer identified by what once held us captive.

Leave It All Behind

"Brethren, I do not count myself to have apprehended;
but one thing I do, forgetting those things which are
behind and reaching forward to those things which
are ahead..."
— Philippians 3:13

We have to grow in our confidence in God's Word. Otherwise, we will always be under the scrutiny of what our past tells us. Either you really are new or you aren't. Either Jesus' blood washed you clean or it didn't. You will reap the fruit of your beliefs. "As a man thinks in his heart, so is he" (see Prov. 23:7). Do you feel that you will always be afraid because of the traumatizing experiences you had in your past? Then that will be the case! Do you feel you will always be angry because you were hurt or abused? That too will continue to manifest! Your beliefs will be revealed in the way you live your life. I can identify an apple tree when I see bright red apples hanging from its branches. In the same way, I can identify someone being ruled by their past when I see them wallowing in guilt, shame, and condemnation.

What's your limit? When the Word says "all things new," what areas in your life do you automatically exclude? What sin is stronger than Jesus' pure, innocent blood? At what point is His sacrifice no longer enough? What moment in your past, whether it was 10 seconds ago or 10 years ago, disqualifies you from His forgiveness?

In the book of Acts, Peter confronts the Jews about something terrible they had done. Do you know what it was? They nailed Jesus, the only begotten Son of God, to a cross. Peter is bold enough to talk about it. He says, "Hey, by the way, you guys killed the Messiah. You crucified the Lord of Creation. You know, the

One we've all been waiting for? Yeah, He finally showed up, and you murdered Him."

Can you imagine? What would it feel like to realize you crucified the only Son of God? Imagine the guilt and weight of condemnation that they must have felt. The Word says that "when they heard this, they were cut to the heart, and said to Peter and the rest of the apostles, 'Men and brethren, what shall we do?'" (Acts 2:37).

Peter responded, "You killed the Son of God, how could you do anything? You're all doomed to hell. You can never make it right. You murdered the incarnate Deity, and there is no forgiveness left for you!"

Is that what he said? No. Peter's response was much different: "Repent, and let every one of you be baptized in the name of Jesus Christ for the remission of sins; and you shall receive the gift of the Holy Spirit. For the promise is to you and to your children, and to all who are afar off, as many as the Lord our God will call" (Acts 2:38-39).

What!?

They crucified Jesus, and the only thing they had to do was repent (change their mind) and get baptized! How scandalous is this Gospel? They nailed Jesus to a tree, and now they're being forgiven for it? How crazy is that? So now here's the question:

Have you ever done anything worse than crucifying Jesus?

It's a trick question. The answer can be found in the song, "How Deep The Father's Love For Us." The lyrics say, "It was my sin that held Him there." Jesus "was delivered over to death for our sins" (Rom. 4:25 NIV). We are all responsible for the death of Jesus. His blood is on all of our hands. If Peter was able to extend forgiveness to those who were present, what about you? Jesus said it Himself as He hung on the Cross:

> *"Father, forgive them, for they do not know what they do."*
> — *Luke 23:34*

It's clear in Scripture that the reason Jesus came was to forever declare His love for you through the remission of your sins. Do you think He failed? No way! He washed *all* of your sins away. The old is completely gone! You are a new creation.

When God made Adam, Adam didn't have a past. All Adam knew was the breath of God that gave him life. When a child is born into this world, neither do they have a past. They're brand new on this planet! Similarly, when we are born again we are *actually* new creations. We start where He finished. His final breath on the Cross is our first breath into a new life. Through His death and resurrection, He gave us the opportunity to have everlasting life! If we can get our eyes off of our sin and onto His sacrifice, we will experience the radical mercy that's waiting to invade our lives. We need to leave it all behind—our sins, our guilt, our bitterness—and accept Jesus as our all in all! Forgiveness is there, waiting to be received. Now is the time. Today is the day of salvation! (See 2 Cor. 6:2.)

The Past is Gone

So again, it is not our past that counts in God's eyes, but Christ's. Jesus has a clean record. The devil has all of your mistakes on file. His little minions work day and night to accuse you with the evidence of your past. However, God kicked that filing cabinet out the window! He's forgotten about it entirely. If you're being accused and shamed with your past, it's not God! "I, even I, am He who blots out your transgressions for My own sake; and I will not remember your sins" (Is. 43:25).

 I know someone who as a younger man got his girlfriend pregnant. Not wanting to deal with being a young father, he convinced her to have an abortion. The decision they made hung over him for many years, despite his repentance and asking for God's forgiveness. Long after they broke up and went their separate ways, he still carried the guilt from his actions.

Years later, this man and I were having a discussion about abortion with a group of mutual friends, and I noticed him getting very tense. I asked him later what had caused him to be so uncomfortable with the conversation, and he reminded me about his experience with abortion. His response caught me off guard. I realized that despite never repeating the same mistake, he had never moved on. He still treated himself like the teenage kid that had made that terrible decision.

The problem was that how he saw himself was very different from how I saw him. I did not view him according to the things he had done, but by who he was now and the person he had become. I encouraged him to stop viewing himself according to his past and to embrace the truth that he was truly a new creation in Christ. Over the next many months, he decided to partner with the truth that his past had been redeemed by the blood of Jesus, and he was no longer the man who made those mistakes.

Later, he and I found ourselves in a similar situation, with a different group of people discussing abortion. However, this time, he was not bothered by the conversation. He was able to talk about the subject without shame or condemnation. His identity in Christ had overtaken his past identity.

Many people struggle with emotional issues stemming from problems of the past. While we cannot change the consequences of our actions, we do not have to live with guilt. God wants you to be free! He doesn't want to simply set you back to "normal." His redemption reaches even farther. He recreates us so that we can walk in Christ as His hands and feet on the earth, meaning we have no painful attachment to our old life. God's salvation is not about sticking it out until we get to heaven. He wants you to release heaven on earth right now! He completely set you free from your past so that you can be defined by Christ and Christ alone.

Whatever your past may be, good or bad, it all comes under the blood of Jesus when you are born again. Our lives are now hidden with Christ in God, which means that when God looks at us, He sees Christ's redemption covering our mistakes. It's time to stop letting our past mistakes disqualify us from receiving the truth of God's love! Receive His mercy and leave the past where it belongs—behind you!

> *"...you have put off the old self with its practices and have put on the new self, which is being renewed in knowledge after the image of its creator."*
> *— Colossians 3:9-10 (ESV)*

Chapter Three

All By Grace

Years ago I heard the testimony of a man who had been battling AIDS for a long time. One day while watching TV, he came across a well-known pastor preaching a sermon. The message impacted him so much that he sent the ministry a donation, requesting a series on healing. When the ministry's secretary received this man's request, she asked the pastor which series she should send him. The pastor thought for a moment and then told her to send him a message on identity and grace.

When the man received the teaching series on identity instead of healing, he was angry. After all, he had given them money. Who were they to not send him what he asked for? So, he took the teachings, tossed them on a shelf somewhere, and forgot about them. A few years later, the man purchased a new home. As he was packing up his things, he came across the teaching series.

By then, he had moved past his offense at the pastor and the ministry, so he decided to give the series a try. As he listened, the power of God touched his body, and he knew something had changed with his condition. He went in to be tested for AIDS again, and not only did he no longer have AIDS, but he wasn't even HIV positive!

What's the point of this story? This man wanted a series on healing so he could learn about the solution to the problem he had. But God had a different plan. His plan was to give the man a revelation of his identity in Christ and the grace of God, and through that, set him free! Through the revelation of God's grace working on his behalf, the man was completely healed.

Are there areas of your life where you have tried to find a solution on your own with no success? Are there places where you consistently come up short and nothing you do ever seems good enough? What if the solution is not in trying again, trying harder, hitting it from a different angle, or figuring out what you did wrong? What if the real solution was much simpler and much more offensive? What if the real way out was to stop striving? It's time to stop trying in our own strength and start surrendering to God's grace.

Our Inheritance

"Now I commit you to God and to the word of his grace, which can build you up and give you an inheritance among all those who are sanctified."
— Acts 20:32 (NASB)

As sons and daughters of God, we have been given an inheritance. It's not an inheritance locked away in a heavenly vault. It's been placed within us, "...that you may know what is the hope of His calling, what are the riches of the glory of His inheritance *in* the saints..." (Eph. 1:18, emphasis added).

Everything God has to offer has already been deposited within our spirits. We can't access it through our works—Bible reading, praying, fasting—we have to access it by grace!

In the natural world, how is an inheritance acquired? If a prince is to inherit the throne of his father's kingdom, what has to happen? His father must die. In order for the last will and testament of any man or woman to go into effect, they must first pass away. "Now when someone leaves a will, it is necessary to prove that the person who made it is dead. The will goes into effect only after the person's death. While the person who made it is still alive, the will cannot be put into effect" (Heb. 9:16-17, NLT). Only then can the inheritance be distributed—not because of anything the beneficiary did, but because of something outside of themselves entirely.

When Jesus died, the will of the Father went into full effect. Once and for all, the way into the Holy of Holies was opened, and the riches of God's inheritance were made accessible to any who would call on His name. Through the blood of Christ, we have been freely given every spiritual blessing in the heavenly places (see Eph. 1:3). We could never attain these things in our flesh! In Christ, by His grace, we have been given *all things*. We are heirs with Christ! Now, through our relationship with Him, we can taste and see the exceeding riches of His kindness toward us.

"Now we have received, not the spirit of the world, but the Spirit who is from God, that we might know the things that have been freely given to us by God."
— 1 Corinthians 2:12

Do You Want to Be Made Well?

John 5 records the story of a paralyzed man by the pool of Bethesda. It was not an unusual sight to see a sick person near the pool. Many came in hopes of a supernatural healing. The story goes that at certain times an angel would come and stir the waters of the pool of Bethesda, and when it did, the first person to enter the waters would be made well.

This particular man had been lying by the pool for 38 years waiting for his chance to crawl down to the waters. Many times the water had been stirred and, in the midst of commotion that followed as people scrambled to jump in the water, he had laid there helpless, asking for someone to help him get in.

When Jesus saw the man lying there, He asked him a simple question, "Do you want to be made well?" However, He did not get a simple answer. Instead of answering yes or no, the man began to share his long story of trying to make it into the pool but never succeeding since he was paralyzed.

Trying and failing had become a habit in this man's life, and it seemed that his only hope was to keep trying the one thing he knew: getting into the pool. Fortunately, Jesus stood before this paralyzed man, uninterested in his merits, strengths, or abilities. His healing had come, not in the form of a ritual or ceremony, but in the form of a Man. Grace personified had come to set this man free from his limitations. He wouldn't have to be stuck in the cycle of trying, failing, and trying harder. He could stop his striving and rely on Jesus.

What this story illustrates is the profound difference between the law and grace. On one side, we have a pool that provides healing under the condition that you must be the first to enter into it.

"*If* I enter the pool when the water is stirred, *then* I will be healed."

The problem with this system, as we can see throughout the Old Testament, is that people were not able to maintain God's standards. They consistently failed to measure up to their side of the covenant. But fortunately, God did not stop at giving us a system of right and wrong; He provided a sacrifice for us in Jesus! Jesus fulfilled the law's requirements in our place, so we can enter into a relationship with God and receive all its benefits through faith in Him.

This man by the pool worked harder and harder and found that his goal slipped farther and farther away. He could not achieve in his own efforts what he was physically incapable of reaching. He couldn't act in opposition to his current state of being. He needed a permanent solution! He found himself at the feet of Jesus, longing for a new start. This was the perfect place for him to be. Jesus' offer was not to help him find a better way to get into the pool, but to show him that his healing was a product of grace. The way out was not through trying harder, but through stopping all of his efforts and choosing to receive God's love.

The beautiful thing is that "God demonstrates His own love toward us, in that while we were still sinners, Christ died for us" (Rom. 5:8). Jesus did not demand us to be clean and perfect or for us to have the ability to do the right thing. He sought us out in our fallen state to restore us in a way that we could never do for ourselves.

Jesus is the image of grace, the embodiment of undeserved favor and goodness, and yet many of us still interact with Him as if He is looking to see how good we have been. Jesus is not Santa Claus. He doesn't give us gifts when we've been good and lumps of coal when we've been bad. He is eternally and unreasonably kind to us as His children.

Prodigal Love

Jesus asked the man by the pool one simple question: "Do you want to be healed?" He wasn't starting a theological debate or a discussion about the secrets of how the pool worked. Jesus was not looking for an explanation for why the man wasn't already healed. He was addressing the man's heart. Do you *want* to be healed?

Many of us respond similarly when Jesus comes to us today. We answer with an excuse or an explanation for why we have not yet experienced something. However, He isn't interested in *why* we aren't experiencing what we wish we were. He simply wants to know *if* we want wholeness. It's not, "Why aren't you healed? Why aren't you prosperous?" Jesus isn't asking those questions. He's asking, "What do you want?" If we want something that is just, pure, and true, He desires to give it to us. He has already paid the price for our newness, and it is ours today if we will only receive it. No matter what obstacle lays in our path, we too, like the paralyzed man, can rise up and walk.

In Luke 15, Jesus used a parable of a wayward son to paint a picture of our radical Father willing to abundantly bless us when we do not deserve it. Much has been said about the prodigal son, but the real power in the story is in the radical measures the father took to express acceptance and love to a son who had harshly rejected him. When the son "was still a great way off, his father saw him and had compassion, and ran" to meet him (verse 20). The father welcomed his lost son home with a ring and a robe, restoring his identity, and killed the fattened calf to celebrate with a feast.

We must move beyond the place where we interact with the Lord on the basis of merit. He is not interested in our righteous deeds apart from our belief in Jesus. Grace came seeking us at the greatest cost, Jesus' blood, and now we can freely receive what we could never earn apart from Him. We cannot live moral and upright lives without first trusting in Jesus. We cannot earn salvation any more than the paralyzed man could enter the pool by himself. Yet, Jesus gives freely what we are unable to accomplish on our own.

He's Done it All

The Christian life has been poorly presented as a method of behavior modification. We think, "Maybe if I do differently, I will become different." While this mentality does have a certain appeal, it cannot produce lasting fruit. Striving to change who we are by changing our actions can be tempting because we rely only on ourselves and can hide our weaknesses. However, you cannot truly change your life by changing your behavior alone. The truth is, we can only consistently "do" what we "are." We can try to change our actions all we want, but the cycles of sin and frustration will never end until we change our hearts. Nothing can change on the outside if we haven't first been renewed on the inside. The inward change always precedes the outward.

It's time for us to recognize that the Lord doesn't want to interact with us based on our ability to act correctly. Many of us mistakenly think God cares more about what we do rather than why we do it. However, He longs for a relationship with us first, and this is where true righteous living springs from. He initiates and pursues, and He provides us the grace we need to be transformed. No matter what our failures say, Jesus' death paid the price for us to have communion with Him.

A Heart of Flesh

Throughout the Old Testament, we see God's promises to remake the heart of man. Ezekiel 36:26-27 says, "I will give you a new heart and put a new spirit within you; I will take the heart of stone out of your flesh and give you a heart of flesh. I will put My Spirit within you and cause you to walk in My statutes, and you will keep My judgments and do them." Ezekiel prophesied a day when God would solve the problem of man's sin at its root, making man into a new creation. This promise of union with the Spirit of God brought hope to a people who were weary of trying to keep the judgments (commandments) of God in order to be in His presence. It would mean that the Law would no longer be necessary because they would not need to modify their behavior to be holy. They would be holy and pure in heart because the Spirit of holiness would live in them.

Jesus fulfilled the promises God made to His chosen people for centuries. He took on the weight of sin so it would no longer hold us back from receiving God's perfect love. He crossed the chasms we had created through our failures and offered us a new birth by believing in Him. We have been given new hearts of flesh by the Holy Spirit. Our hearts have been made new! Even if you do not see this as a present reality, you must anchor yourself in the all-accomplishing work of Jesus Christ. He who promised is faithful. He *has* made all things new!

Messy Rooms and Whitewashed Tombs

As kids, most of us probably had an experience (or one similar) where we pushed all of our toys, junk, and dirty clothes under our beds in order to hide the mess from our parents. In our young minds, the room was spotless! Not a single pair of dirty socks could be seen! We could lay on top of our beds in total bliss, thinking our parents would never know. However, before long, the truth would come out one way or another. Mom or Dad would find our hidden messes (or smell them) and expose the reality. The room was never really clean; it was all a façade. This childish behavior is exactly what the Pharisees were exposed for.

Jesus called the Pharisees "whitewashed tombs." He confronted them for painstakingly maintaining a flawless external appearance while neglecting what truly matters: the heart! He despised their hypocrisy, seeing their "holy living" as prideful attempts to earn right-standing with God and look better than everyone else. Their appearance of holiness was a sham. It did not come from God, the author of holiness. It did not proceed from the heart.

Unlike the Pharisees who worked from the outside-in, we live from the inside-out, and thus we can be sure we will manifest righteousness in action (newness) in due time. Jesus told the Pharisees, "First cleanse the inside of the cup and dish, that the outside of them may be clean also" (Matt. 23:26). We have the Holy Spirit Himself living in us, and He will clean the inside of our hearts. He is our guarantee for perfection, newness, and complete redemption as sons and daughters (see Eph. 1:14). We can have confidence that all things in our life *will* be made new because we *have* been made new.

Better Than Before

One of my pastor friends told me a story about how one of his sons had always wanted a very nice, expensive sports car. So one year for his birthday, the pastor went out and bought his son the car as a surprise. His son was so excited and thankful to his father for giving him such a generous gift.

A few months later, the pastor got a call from his son late at night. He was in tears because he had taken a joy ride, lost control, and wrecked the car. His father quickly left his home and drove to the scene of the accident. Upon arrival, he realized the car wasn't just wrecked. It was totaled. As he listened, his son wept, confessing that he had been driving recklessly and acting irresponsibly.

The father patiently listened to his son confess but didn't say much. After his son finished sharing, the father forgave him and told him not to worry and that everything would work out. He said he would take him to the car dealership and get him an even better car than the one he had just totaled.

Wait, what? What kind of parenting is that?

This is actually a true story. It sounds counterintuitive, right? Maybe a little too extreme? After all, why would anyone buy a more expensive car for someone who had just shown they couldn't handle the first one? How else would his son know what he did was wrong if there was no punishment for his actions? From a worldly perspective, that seems wasteful and irresponsible. However, this is exactly how grace operates in our lives. Our worldly experience teaches us that second chances are rare and must be earned. Even when they come, we hear, "You better get it right this time!" But that's not the

Gospel. Radical mercy and extravagant grace define the attitude of the Kingdom.

Mercy and Grace

We often make the mistake of thinking that the words "mercy" and "grace" can be used interchangeably to mean "not getting what we deserve." This is a good definition of mercy, but it falls short of capturing the character of grace. Grace is the power of God to create change in our lives. It restores us to a place *better* than where we were when we fell. Mercy is when we don't get the punishment we deserve. Grace, however, is when we get a blessing or reward that we *don't* deserve. Mercy releases us from our wrong-doing. Grace blesses us despite our wrong-doing.

Imagine you are walking up a flight of stairs and you suddenly trip and fall back down to the bottom. To get back to the top, you would have to start all over again climbing up the stairs. However, if the same thing happened on an escalator, by the time you got back up, you would already be at the top. The escalator would continue to carry you even during your recovery. This might sound like a silly example, but it does illustrate how grace works in and through us. In issues of sin, we still face consequences for our behavior, but God is ready and willing to redeem the effects of our sin when we turn to Him in repentance.

Even on our worst days, under grace, we are still moving forward, being ever-increasingly transformed into the image of Christ. This is not because of our inherent goodness or character; it is a result of God's power working in our lives. Grace, in short, is the power of God operating in us to bring us into the image and likeness of God. It operates through us, often despite of us, and cannot be stopped. The basic requirement to receive it is this: believe (see John 6:29).

Divinely Changed

A divine exchange took place at the Cross. Jesus, the perfect Son of God, became sin on our behalf so that we could take on His righteousness. He became poor so that we could become rich. He was rejected so that we could be accepted. He was humiliated so that we could be exalted. He was condemned as a criminal so that we could be set free. Whatever is true of Jesus is true of us. Therefore, God treats us according to what Jesus deserves and *not* to what we deserve. So there's no point in looking back on our qualifications or failures. Neither of these matter in God's eyes. All God sees in us is Christ, and because of Christ, we are the object of His desire and affections.

We are no longer mere human beings (see 1 Cor. 3:3). We have been made one with Christ, becoming something new the world has never seen. We must move beyond the worldly system of merits, demerits, "do-good-get-good," "do-bad-get-bad." We must recognize that God's measuring stick for our lives is now Christ and Christ alone. We can neither remove ourselves from His good graces nor earn extra credit. Jesus has credited our accounts far more than we ever could have on our own. We couldn't possibly pay off the debts of our sins—Christ did it for us! How could we, in our humanity, fix the hearts we broke? How could we possibly restore the joy we took from someone? All the hurt we have caused the people around us, Christ is ready to heal. He is ready to bring justice to those we have spiritually and physically stolen from. That's the power of His forgiveness. It goes beyond our ability to "make things right." It ripples into the lives of those that have been affected by our shortcomings. He has divinely changed you so you can divinely change the world. Even the things you could never make up for, He is ready to reconcile. It is time we step beyond the confines of a law-based existence and into the marvelous light and freedom that Jesus' blood bought for us and everyone we know!

Each of us have areas in our lives where we need a touch from the Lord. Today, amid our trials and difficulties, Jesus presents us with the same question He asked the paralyzed man lying by the pool of Bethesda: "Do you want to be made well?" He does not ask us what we have done to become well, whether or not we deserve to be well, or what we are going to do differently in the future to achieve wellness. He simply asks us if we *want* wellness.

The problem with self-righteousness is that it keeps us so focused on what *we* are doing and how *we* can improve ourselves, leaving very little room for Jesus to come and give us His grace. Jesus will not bless self-effort. He gives grace to those who are humble and to those who recognize their emptiness and need to be filled. It is time to let go and move on from trying to earn righteousness and simply let Him love you. It is *His* kindness that leads us to repentance (changing how we see and think), and *His* grace that causes us to "have an abundance for every good work" (2 Cor. 9:8). However, we cannot receive from Him if our hands are "full" of our own works.

Our works are what we can do in our own strength, apart from faith. They are our attempts to achieve a goal without resting in Christ first and relying on Him to move through us. Jesus says, "Come to Me, all you who labor and are heavy laden, and I will give you rest" (Matt. 11:28). He tells us to take His yoke upon us and that we will find rest. "For My yoke is easy and My burden is light" (verse 30).

Today, choose to lay your burdens down at His feet and let Him work on your behalf. This is not to say we never labor, but resting in Him is a conscious choice to trust Him, which will naturally result in a changed life. Rest is one of the most powerful tools in the believers belt, but it is oftentimes overlooked. I write more in depth on this in my book *The Lost Art of Rest*. He is the One making all things new, all by His grace. Our transformation is not up to us. He initiates change and leads us into greater things. Let Him remind you of His love for you. He cares about your life and the challenges you face much more than you do!

> *"For it pleased the Father that in Him all the fullness*
> *should dwell, and by Him to reconcile all things to*
> *Himself, by Him, whether things on earth or things*
> *in heaven, having made peace through the blood of*
> *His cross."*
>
> *— Colossians 1:19-20*

Part Two

ALL THINGS WORK TOGETHER FOR GOOD

"And we know that all things work together for good to those who love God, to those who are the called according to His purpose."
— Romans 8:28

Chapter Four

If It's Not Good, It's Not Over

In 1501, the great artist and sculptor Michelangelo was commissioned by a church in Florence to make a depiction of King David. As part of a series of sculptures based on the Old Testament prophets, it was to sit atop one of the buttresses of the Florence Cathedral. The statue of King David had been unsuccessfully commissioned twice before. A local quarry had provided a large block of marble, nicknamed "The Giant," for the undertaking. The first sculptor had begun the work with passion but only made it as far as roughly cutting out the shapes of the legs before he lost all hope of ever completing the project.

Another sculptor had come along a few years later attempting to take up the task, but again, quickly became disheartened and hopeless about ever being able to make anything from such a massive piece of stone. The piece of marble Michelangelo inherited to begin his work had sat in the cathedral workshop untouched and unused for nearly 26 years.

"The Giant" was considered by all to be too large and too flawed to ever be made into anything worthy to display.

However, Michelangelo did not believe what others said about the piece of marble. He believed he could succeed where others had failed. For two years, Michelangelo labored day and night in secrecy, carefully removing chunks of marble bit by bit. He worked with unmatched dedication, refusing to stop even when the elements turned against him. When it rained, he would work until his clothes were drenched and too heavy for him to lift his arms. When he slept, he stayed in his work clothes and did not leave his workshop.

In 1504, almost three years later, Michelangelo unveiled his work to the city of Florence. Their reception was far beyond what anyone could have imagined. Though the statue was originally commissioned to sit atop the cathedral, looking down on the city from a height, the council unanimously agreed that the work was too perfect to sit at such a distance where no one would be able to truly appreciate what Michelangelo had accomplished. After much discussion, the council decided that the best place to showcase the statue would be in the Piazza della Signoria, in the heart of the city. King David stood watch over the city in that plaza for over 400 years until it was replaced by a replica in 1873 to protect it from further weathering.

Michelangelo took a slab of stone that sat rejected and abandoned for 26 years due to its imperfections, and he transformed it into one of the greatest masterpieces of all time. Seeing its condition at the start, no one could have imagined what it would become. Michelangelo was able to see past its flaws to its true potential and refused to stop working until the image that stood before him matched what he saw in his mind's eye. One newspaper columnist, Bob Considine, imagined what a conversation between Michelangelo and an admirer would have sounded like:

"'How in God's name could you have achieved a masterpiece like this from a crude slab of marble?' a fan is supposed to have asked him.

'It was easy,' Mike is said to have said. 'All I did was chip away everything that didn't look like David.'"

We should see ourselves with the same hopeful perspective Michelangelo had for his work. What flaws do you see in your own life? What imperfections do you see in yourself that the enemy uses to disqualify you? No matter our imperfections or failures, God, the Master Artist, never stops working on us. He's faithfully chipping away everything that isn't you. He's going to liberate you from the bondage of that heavy, old life. Philippians 1:6 (NASB) says, "For I am confident of this very thing, that He who began a good work in you will perfect it until the day of Christ Jesus." If an area in our lives is not yet a masterpiece, God is not done working.

To put it another way, God is *always* good. Psalm 145:9 says, "The Lord is good to all, and His tender mercies are over all His works." His desire is to restore every area of our lives. Knowing His nature and His will toward us, we can safely say: "If something in my life isn't good, God isn't done!"

Perseverance

Throughout 70 long years of captivity and 70 years of humble service, Daniel, the Old Testament hero, persisted in faith. He persisted because he held onto the promise of God. While a life of captivity in Babylon was all Daniel knew, he took God at His Word and held Him to a promise He had made to Jeremiah almost a century earlier. In his study of the

Scriptures, Daniel read, "These nations shall serve the king of Babylon seventy years" (Jer. 25:11). Doing the math, Daniel discovered that he was living in a special moment in time—it had been exactly 70 years since Israel had been taken captive by Babylon. He was living in the very year God had promised to deliver Israel. Daniel was determined to see God's promise of freedom come to pass.

Today, we have a Bible chock-full of promises! If you know and are convinced that God has good things in store for those who love Him, the same determination will be kindled within you. If you understand that *all* of His promises are "yes," then nothing will keep you from persisting until you see the manifestation of His goodness (see 2 Cor. 1:20).

So, when Daniel discovered God's promise of deliverance, he prayed, "'O Lord, hear! O Lord, forgive! O Lord, listen and act! Do not delay for Your own sake, my God, for Your city and Your people are called by Your name'" (Dan. 9:19). Daniel didn't sit by and wait for the promises of God to come to pass. He took ownership and became a participant in the move of God. He let the Word of God motivate him to act. He knew that even though he and his nation were in bondage, they would soon be set free. God had promised it! This is what motivated Daniel to pray.

Even though his current state of captivity conflicted with where he was called to be, Daniel was not discouraged. He defined his destiny by God's promise instead of his current experience. Although he and his nation served a tyrannical king, were humiliated by slavery, and had been persecuted for following the Lord, he still believed they were God's chosen people. Although Israel's captivity was extended due to their disobedience, we see in chapter 10 that Daniel did not give up. Even when he didn't see fruit from his prayers for 21 days, Daniel continued to pray, remembering the promise that God had given years ago.

Even in the waiting, God was still working for his good! Daniel unknowingly had an archangel assist him in seeing his prayers fulfilled. God was certainly moving on Daniel's behalf, and although his prayer had no initial evidence of being heard, it was effective! Imagine if Daniel had only prayed to the extent that he saw his prayers working. He very well could have stopped after hour 8, day 5, or day 20... but Daniel did not let what he saw (or didn't see) affect his actions. He was confident in what God had spoken.

Daniel had plenty of evidence of God's goodness to persist even when he didn't see immediate results. He is just one of many heroes in the Bible who modeled persevering faith (check out my book *Never Give Up* for an in-depth teaching on this subject). Time and time again, we see these generals model persistent faith even through extremely difficult situations. We must do the same today.

When we believe that God is doing great things even during times of hardship, we will take action to partner with Him, just like Daniel did. True faith leads to action. Perseverance is the fruit of taking God at His word. It says, "I won't stop until I see good come from this because God has made a promise." Just like Michelangelo persisting with his masterpiece, God is persisting with us. Those who persevere through trials trust that "He who promised is faithful" (Heb. 10:23). They know that God will come through because they've seen Him do it before. We must know that if a circumstance isn't good, then God isn't finished, and we shouldn't be either.

We must be so convinced that God's plan for us is prosperity (see Jer. 29:11) that we continue to trust Him until it comes to fruition in our lives. We must stand firm in the goodness of God, knowing that He wants us to live in the manifestation of His nature. This belief will cause us to have hope no matter how hopeless a circumstance may be. No matter where we find ourselves, God is faithful. He still has a plan and is not only capable of working all things together for our good but is eager to do so as well. This assurance of God's nature gives us a bigger perspective when we face challenging circumstances. It allows us to trust God, knowing that He is working in, through, and all around us.

God desires to right *all* the wrongs in our lives. How can I be so sure of this? Because Jesus already paid the price! He came to bring perfect justice. Any area of your life that has been robbed, whether it be a relationship, a work situation, or a health issue, has been redeemed in full through the blood of Christ. It's through our knowledge of Him that we access and experience His provision of "all things" pertaining to life and godliness (see 2 Peter 1:3). It's the devil that "does not come except to steal, and to kill, and to destroy." Jesus came "that [we] may have life, and that [we] may have it more abundantly" (John 10:10). Jesus took our sin and its effects on Himself when He died on the Cross, purchasing a victorious, abundant, and brand new life for us. This means that He has accomplished ultimate redemption, so we can see redemption throughout our lives.

But you don't understand. I did this to myself! I put myself in debt. I made myself sick. I ruined this relationship!

Okay, but do you wish you hadn't? An inspiring friend of mine, Dan Mohler, once said, "The moment you wish you hadn't is the moment you're no longer the person who did." That's the power of repentance! The moment you change your mind, turn from your sin, and realize there's a greater way, is the moment mercy comes in and makes all things new. It is just like the Jews who had crucified Jesus. Once they realized their error, they repented, got baptized, and received the inheritance of God's Holy Spirit. Praise God for His redemption!

"I'm Here To Forgive You"

One of the most rewarding things I get to do is lead ministry trips all over the world. Almost every year since 2000, I have taken a team to South Africa for a jam-packed mission trip. We go everywhere from prisons to government meetings, slums to businesses, and hospitals to schools. The people who come on these trips see incredible miracles, and when we debrief each night, the stories we hear are mind-blowing.

In 2018, one of our students, Zach, left his backpack in the backseat of a car while the team walked the streets of an impoverished South African neighborhood, or "township." About an hour into ministry, our local guide received a phone call from the church where they had left the car. Someone had broken in and taken his backpack, which contained several expensive items and his favorite Bible.

The pastor, following a hunch about who had done this, immediately started working to find the thief. Despite the situation, Zach continued to minister with his team and saw God move powerfully in the nearby homes. He saw the situation for what it was—a distraction that could have interrupted a day's ministry. He knew that good would come from the situation. He believed and declared, "I'm going to get my backpack back."

Hearing the story later, what struck me was Zach's reaction to a circumstance that could have been very discouraging. He had many valuable things in his backpack. However, all he wanted was the opportunity to look the thief in the eye, forgive him, and preach the Gospel to him.

Zach was not as concerned with reclaiming his belongings as he was with the criminal experiencing the transformational love of Jesus. His perspective was not on his material loss but on the soul of the person who had committed the crime. Zach knew that God works all things for good, so he looked forward to a resolution even beyond his own good. When we live with this perspective and trust in the Lord as our source, I believe He will bring about that which we desire and work for the good of everyone involved.

A few days later, the police called me saying they had apprehended the person responsible for breaking into the car and stealing the bag. Zach rode with one of our host pastors, not only to reclaim his belongings, but also in hopes of meeting the person responsible. When he arrived at the prison, he briefly discussed the list of belongings that had been stolen, but he emphasized his desire to meet the person responsible. He said of this situation, "I knew God had me there for another reason. I wanted to go speak with the person who stole my bag, forgive him, and tell him about Jesus."

The prison administrator was willing to let him see the young man and led Zach and the rest of his team back to the cell door. There they met the thief, a boy who was only 16 years old. His head was hung low, and tears rolled down his cheeks as he considered how his life might be different from this moment on. He clearly regretted what he had done, and he felt so sorry that he couldn't even look Zach in the eye. However, Zach told him, "I'm not here to press charges against you. I'm here to forgive you." As he repeated these words and shared the Good News of Jesus' extravagant forgiveness and mercy, the expression on the boy's face slowly turned from fear and sadness into shock and unbelief. He was stunned and did not understand why someone would forgive him. The mercy Zach showed was so unexpected, yet so relieving. In response, the boy gave his life to Jesus! As Zach embraced him, the boys' tears stained his shirt. They knew he would never be the same.

Imagine what might have happened if Zach had decided to press charges against the boy for what he had done. He had every "right" to, after all. But Zach knew the circumstance wouldn't only work out for his good but for the good of the perpetrator as well. Because Zach had that revelation, he acted on it by showing God's mercy. God will take even the worst circumstances and turn them around for the good of those who love Him.

Zach retrieved all of the most valuable items in his bag, including expensive electronics and his watch. However, he didn't receive back the possession he wanted the most: his Bible. At first, this was hard for him, but he quickly got over it and realized that this was no accident. More than likely, that Bible became someone else's precious possession. Zach knew the life of the person who stole the Bible was so much more important than the Bible itself. Through the process, the Lord showed him that this moment marked a new start, a season of knowing God's power of redemption more deeply and receiving new revelation from the Word. His understanding of God's redemptive love expanded as he realized it meant far more to him than ever before.

A Lesson from Science

Here's an analogy to further illustrate God's ability to take our messy situations and work them for our good. In chemistry, Sodium (Na) and Chlorine (Cl) are both extremely volatile and dangerous substances. Sodium is a metal that is so reactive that when exposed to even a little water, it will combust and explode. It must be kept in an oil solution at all times to keep it from rapidly oxidizing. Chlorine, on the other hand, is a poisonous gas that can be fatal if inhaled in large enough quantities.

However, if you combine these two substances you get table salt (NaCl), which is vital to our body's health and enhances our food's taste. I find it interesting that the Lord made a common household item out of two individually deadly elements.

This is who God is! He calls those things which are dead back to life. He pieces our circumstances together like a puzzle, revealing a final image that glorifies His name. He is so good that He can even take things that are harmful or dangerous and use them to create something purposeful and beneficial. He is the author of all good things and creates good in our lives no matter the situation. Perhaps today there are things in your life that threaten your peace or are causing you to lose hope. However, don't lose sight of God and His goodness. Let me encourage you again that if it's not good yet, then God is not finished.

God Has a Plan

When I was 18 years old, my dad had a massive stroke. The doctors gave him only two days to live. I was devastated. In an instant, everything seemed to collapse around me. My dad pushed through, to the amazement of the doctors, yet death seemed to linger in my family for the next two years as he fought to recover. In the months to come, my aunt died from cancer. My uncle died from cancer. One of my best friends was deported. My dog strangled itself to death on its leash. I was in two major car accidents. Everything that could go wrong went wrong. Pain, heartache, and confusion seemed to surround and taunt me. As my dad continued the fight for survival and the world seemed to be burning around me, there was one thing that kept me going. I knew God had a plan for me, and I knew my future would be bright.

When I was 20 years old, my dad passed away. It was the climax to the hardest two years of my life. Despite the devastation, I set my eyes on Jesus and continued to move forward. The next three months were extremely difficult. Toward the end of this time, I felt the Lord say, "Either you will conquer this, or this is going to conquer you." Through it all, I was set on fire with a conviction to see the sick healed. Even though my dad was taken by a stroke, I was convinced I would see sickness, disease, and pain bow to the name of Jesus. Sure enough, that's exactly what I began to witness. What the enemy meant for evil actually inspired me to conquer, thrive, and establish God's Kingdom. To this day I have seen thousands of people healed through the power of Jesus Christ. Even the very ailment that took my father I have seen bow at the feet of Jesus!

During hard times, it is especially important to stay anchored in Christ and who He is in us. If we focus on ourselves and the pain we feel, we can be consumed by it. However, selflessness is the sure way to maintain a healthy perspective in any circumstance. We must remember that our lives are not our own and that we bring God glory by staying steadfast through trials. While it may not be "good" right now, focus on Jesus, letting His presence bring you peace, and all things will fall into the right perspective.

No matter what you may be struggling with, know that God still has a good plan for you and will redeem every hard circumstance. Not only will you come through, but you will come out ahead! God's grace will meet us where our natural ability ends and will propel us farther than we could ever go on our own. God always works all things together for the good of those who love Him and are called according to His purpose.

*"For I consider that the sufferings of this present time
are not worthy to be compared with the glory which
shall be revealed in us."*
— Romans 8:18

Chapter Five

Inconvenient Favor

Christ became one with our sufferings and came out victorious. There's no inconvenient circumstance you could ever face that's bigger than the victory of Jesus' life, death, and resurrection. Christ became poor so we could become rich. He became sin so we could become His righteousness. He became a curse so we could be blessed.

As I've mentioned, there was a season when I studied the Word to discover the rewards of Christ's death in our place. While I was learning about how amazing and complete this divine exchange is, I came across Luke 2:52, "And Jesus increased in wisdom and stature, and in favor with God and men." I asked the Lord how I could apply this verse to my life, and I heard Him say, "Jesus grew in favor with God and man so you can walk in the fullness of favor that He already grew in." It was at that point that I realized my ability and the favor I walk in has nothing to do with me but everything to do with Jesus.

From Bad to Blessed

As an itinerant minister, I travel frequently. I have been to over 35 countries and spoken in countless cities and churches. As you can imagine, traveling long distances, especially with a large team, seldom goes exactly as planned. Everywhere I go, I constantly find myself in situations where things don't go smoothly, but here's the thing: I end up blessed because of it.

On one trip back from Europe, my checked bag got "lost" somewhere in transit. There was no trace of it. Since I was a frequent flyer with the airline, they gave me a voucher to purchase anything I needed to replace the items in the lost bag. They told me I could spend up to $1,500 to replace what was lost as compensation for the unusual situation.

That week I went on a shopping spree, buying new shoes, a new jacket, a new bag, and new toiletries to replace what had been lost. At the end of the week, I sent them all the receipts for the items I had purchased and went about my business. One month later the airline called me saying they had found my bag in an Eastern European country that I had not visited, and the bag was being shipped to me. When it arrived, all of my original belongings were untouched and nothing was missing. At the expense of having to go without my bag for a week and a half, I had recovered all of my belongings and $1,500 worth of brand new clothes and items as well!

This is just one of the countless times I've received extraordinary favor at the expense of a momentary inconvenience. I have coined these all-too-common situations as "inconvenient favor." When people ask me why I am blessed so often with inconvenient favor, I tell them it's because of the outlook I've learned to have when things seem to go wrong.

Whenever I experience an inconvenience, I expect something good to come out of it.

The value of these situations is not limited to the material blessings received from less-than-satisfactory circumstances. They have taught me a greater truth about God's nature and how He interacts with us in the midst of trials. He wants to bless us abundantly, and He will work frustrating situations for our good in order to do so.

When things aren't going as planned or problems arise, I get excited. I start looking for the hand of the Lord, anticipating His power to right the wrongs. Not only that, but I also look for the ways that He could bring even greater good to the situation. It may sound crazy to you, but I don't have to hope things will work out anymore. I *know* that all things are going to work together for my good and that whenever plans are delayed or unexpected problems arise, blessings are on their way to me.

Romans 8:28 says, "And we know that *all things* work together for good to those who love God, to those who are the called according to His purpose." How do you handle setbacks in your own life? Do you live with similar confidence in the Lord's work? Do you believe that no matter the situation, He will come through on His word? Do you live with an expectation that blessing is waiting for you on the other side of trial?

The book of James opens with this incredible exhortation: "My brethren, count it all joy when you fall into various trials, knowing that the testing of your faith produces patience. But let patience have its perfect work, that you may be perfect and complete, lacking nothing" (James 1:2-4). God *wants* you to rejoice in trials, not because trials are fun or praiseworthy on their own, but because of what He will orchestrate in your life through them. He wants you to take on a higher perspective of your circumstances, to be excited about how He will come through for you. All things work together for good, no matter how bad, how hard, or how inconvenient.

He Turns the Bitter into Sweet

In Moses' time, when the Israelites had marched their way out of bondage in Egypt, the people of God encountered a bitter situation. They came to a place in the wilderness where the only available water was sour and undrinkable.

> *"Now when they came to Marah, they could not drink the waters of Marah, for they were bitter. Therefore the name of it was called Marah. And the people complained against Moses, saying, 'What shall we drink?'"*
> *— Exodus 15:23-24*

Many of us encounter times in our lives where we ask ourselves the same question: "What will we drink? What can we possibly do with this financial situation? What could ever be done about this broken relationship? How could this sickness ever be cured?" It's normal to ask these types of questions. However, God's reality is far superior and far beyond "normal"! He jumps into the bitter waters of our lives, meets us where we are, and turns our world upside down.

> *"So he cried out to the Lord, and the Lord showed him a tree. When he cast it into the waters, the waters were made sweet..."*
> *— Exodus 15:25*

How amazing is that? Moses took a tree, representing the Cross of Jesus Christ, and threw it into the waters of Marah!

God took His only Son and sent Him into the dead-center of our bitterness. He became sin at the Cross, and He conquered death three days later. Every bitter situation has been given an antidote—the victory of Jesus Christ. When things get bitter, turn to the Cross. Allow Him to make your life sweeter than it could ever be on your own! Don't run from your bitter waters allow Jesus to step in and change it for good!

Always Faithful

God has been very faithful to me in the area of finances. I consider myself a blessed person, and I do not let money become a limitation when I make decisions. I love getting to show generosity toward others! It's a great way to live life. However, I was not always able to do what I do now. In fact, in the early years of starting Grace Place, I did not have much money at all.

I remember one week, in particular, I checked to see how much money I had. I only had $38 in the bank and $2 in my pocket. I did not have another speaking engagement coming for a while and I had no other means of income. To put it simply, I was broke. That night I was meeting the young men I was mentoring for "Family Night," a weekly gathering we hold in Grace Place. We get together for a meal, a time of worship, a message, and ministry time. Every week for Family Night, all the young men would pitch in for food, and we would eat together and share about our week. It would have been easy, given my financial position, to let them each pay their share as normal. However, that night, I knew I needed to do something to declare that I wasn't a hostage to my bank account. I used all $40 to buy dinner that night. When the time came to collect money, I told them to keep it. This week's meal was on me.

We had a great night together. We talked, laughed, and I taught on identity in Christ. Going home that night, I laughed out loud, thinking, "Lord, you're going to have to do something." I didn't let myself worry about my finances. I didn't know how, but I trusted that God was going to show up and provide for me. I stopped by the mailbox on my way into the house and was surprised to find a letter from a major franchise coffee shop I had previously worked for. It had been a few years since I worked for them, and I hadn't received mail from them in some time. The letter stated that they had been reviewing their employee accounts and realized that they had not paid me for all of the hours I had worked. They had enclosed a check for $768!

While I worked there, I was meticulous about tracking my hours and reviewing my paychecks. If anything was off, I would let them know. For that reason, this money came as a surprise. God had chosen to bless me through my former employer. I knew this was in response to my willingness to give my last $40 away instead of holding onto it for myself. That day, I had a very clear choice to either partner with fear and hopelessness or with the Lord in truth. I firmly believe that had I chosen to partner with fear, I would not have found that check in my mailbox that night.

When God promises to work all things together for our good, we must understand that His definition of goodness far exceeds our own. God didn't see me give $40 and then give me back $40. He provided far above and beyond my starting point. He does not give in equal measure to our giving. Abundance is His desire for all of us. Please understand this doesn't just apply to money. This is a spiritual principle that is written into His nature. He wants us to understand what He is like, and He reveals His nature through displaying His goodness in situations like this.

According to His Purpose

The story of Joseph in the Old Testament is one of the greatest displays of God turning all things for good. In Genesis 37, Joseph dreamt of greatness. He knew that one day he would have influence over many people, even his own family. However, in the process, he was thrown into a pit by his brothers and left for dead. In a moment of hesitation, they sold him into slavery instead. He was taken away from his family and his homeland. This seems like the opposite of Joseph's dream! As a slave in Egypt, he was wrongly accused of rape, arrested, and left in prison for years. He was met with so much opposition, and yet he maintained his character and integrity. He trusted in the faithfulness of God.

If Joseph thought the same way many Christians do today, he would have had every reason to lose hope in God's goodness and the fulfillment of his dreams. However, instead of resorting to a hopeless perspective, he maintained a faith in God that was richly rewarded. While in prison, the warden put Joseph in charge of all the other prisoners and over everything that happened in the prison (see Gen. 39:22). When he was eventually released, he was immediately promoted to the head over multitudes. Pharaoh said to him, "'You shall be over my house, and all my people shall be ruled according to your word; only in regard to the throne will I be greater than you.' And Pharaoh said to Joseph, 'See, I have set you over all the land of Egypt'" (Gen. 41:40-41).

Joseph not only grew in the influence and favor he had dreamt of as a young man, but he became second-in-command over the most powerful nation on the earth at the time! To completely rewrite the wrongs done to him, he provided for the very brothers that left him for dead. Because of his God-given wisdom, his whole family and an entire nation were preserved. God redeemed every detail of his story, fulfilling the intention He'd always had to prosper Joseph.

After their father Jacob died, Joseph's brothers came to him begging for mercy, afraid that he would retaliate against them for the evil they had committed against him in his youth. However, Joseph's response to their plea for mercy reveals his perspective and trust in the Lord and His plan: "You meant evil against me, but God meant it for good in order to bring about this present result, to keep many people alive" (Gen. 50:20 NASB). Joseph knew that God always works even the worst situations for our good because He has good plans for us.

God accomplished His purposes through Joseph's life. Not only did He rewrite Joseph's story with a happy ending, but He also rewrote the story of the entire nation of Israel. His chosen people survived a famine that would have otherwise destroyed them because of the influence and wisdom God gave Joseph. He was called according to God's purposes, and God made a way for ultimate good to come out of his story, making him a key figure in the history of Israel.

Every single thing is working together for not only our good but the good of all who love God and are "called according to His purpose." This must become a core belief for us, leading us to expect good any time something negative comes along. The hope of resolution and abundant blessing will lead us to persevere even when obstacles come our way. This expectation of good puts us in the position to receive an abundance of favor through any storm we may face.

Exceedingly Abundantly

No matter what life throws at us, we can rest assured that God will turn it around for the good of His Kingdom and for the good of His children. His will for us is to experience goodness in the land of the living (see Psalm 27:13), and this goodness is "exceedingly abundantly above all that we ask or think" (Eph. 3:20). God wants us to thrive, not just survive.

Too many believers are living with an incorrect perception of God and His goodness. We read Scriptures like Romans 8:28 and think that "good" can include situations that God would never consider good. His will is for us to live in peace and abundance spiritually, emotionally, physically, financially, and relationally. In Galatians 5:1 (NIV), Paul writes that "it is for freedom that Christ has set us free..." God wants us to enjoy life and live in freedom, and Christ paid the price for us to live in that freedom!

Some of us have been taught that hardships like sickness and poverty are parts of life we must simply endure. However, they are not God's will for us! Jeremiah 29:11 (NIV) says, "'For I know the plans I have for you,' declares the LORD, 'plans to prosper you and not to harm you, plans to give you hope and a future.'" A verse in 3 John also reveals God's heart for us: "Beloved, I pray that you may prosper in all things and be in health, just as your soul prospers" (3 John 2). Sickness and lack are the opposite of prosperity. God does not wish that for the lives of those He created. Jesus modeled this by healing every sick person that came to Him. He became the solution to the world's problems wherever He went.

God is truly *good*, and He wants us to live in His goodness. "Surely goodness and mercy shall follow [us] all the days of [our lives]..." (Psalm 23:6). When we understand that God is good and that His will for us is good, we will begin to expect good things in every area of life! It is this confidence in the redemption of God that gives us hope for resolution no matter what hardship comes our way. We will have a better outlook on life because we know that if a circumstance is not good, then the story is not over.

God redeems situations that seem to hold us back. And He doesn't stop there—He continues to work situations for our good so that we experience more blessing than we had in the first place! Now let me be very clear. God does not cause negative things to happen. That is not consistent with His nature. He is good, and all good things come from Him (see Ps. 16:2, James 1:17). Sometimes the good that comes from a negative situation can be so good that we might wonder if God caused the bad thing to happen in the first place. His redemption is so complete that He can completely rewrite the outcome of any situation! However, this doesn't mean God caused something to happen. He is an expert at bringing good from even the worst of scenarios. He is the author of good and good alone.

Keep Going

When something challenging comes your way, how do you respond? Are you filled with fear or the expectation of more hardship? We must learn to expect the goodness of God in every situation in order to receive it. Every time we are challenged, it is an opportunity to grow our faith in the goodness and power of God. No matter what comes our way, we are in charge of how we respond. Our eager expectation of good in the face of a negative situation reveals our faith in God.

Life is not a matter of what happens to us, but it is a matter of how we handle it. Anything we face can be turned around for good if we handle it well and continue to trust God through it. Normal life is full of ups and downs, but the Christian life is to go from glory to glory (see 2 Cor. 3:18), continually going up as we get to know Christ more and more. If we combine any situation we face with the hope of God's faithful redemption, nothing will shake our faith. We will know that an "up" is coming if we seem to be experiencing a "down." We will begin to expect that He is always working all things together for our good.

> *"In Him also we have obtained an inheritance, being predestined according to the purpose of Him who works all things according to the counsel of His will."*
> — *Ephesians 1:11*

Chapter Six

All for His Glory

A salesman left his house early one morning to drive to another city for a very important meeting with a prospective client. The meeting was several hours away, and he had left a little later than intended. He had no time for a pit stop.

In his rush to leave the house, he hadn't enjoyed his usual morning cup of coffee. Coincidentally, about an hour into the drive, he passed a billboard advertising a popular fast food chain. It featured a large picture of a refreshing iced coffee.

His stomach gave a slight rumble at the thought of how long it would be before he could eat. He knew the meeting had the potential to go on for many hours. It would be nice to get something to eat or drink beforehand. He checked his watch, made a few brief calculations in his head, and decided to make a quick stop at the next exit.

Unfortunately, he had not read the sign correctly when he made his mental calculations. The restaurant was much further from the highway than he thought, and it was very busy. After being at the restaurant for 25 minutes, the man drove back onto the highway, worried how his decision would impact the outcome of the meeting. By the time he arrived at the location, he was 35 minutes late. His client had decided that if this was how his time was going to be treated, then he would prefer to work with someone else. The salesman was turned away empty-handed by the receptionist. Because he turned off for a quick bite to eat, the salesman had missed out on the entire reason he left his house early that morning.

Keep Moving Forward

I often tell those I'm discipling that life is like a highway. We're driving along, headed wherever God is taking us, and we look to the side and see a billboard advertising something at the next exit. If this advertisement is especially appealing, we will exit the highway and no longer continue on the road God has us on. These billboards are the thoughts in our minds that the enemy tries to distract us with. We must look away and keep driving forward to stay on track.

The enemy will use all sorts of thoughts to distract us from where God is calling us to be. He knows that the average Christian will become discouraged, self-focused, and ineffective for Christ during hard times. He uses lies like "you're way ahead of yourself," "take some 'me time'," and "just one little compromise won't make a difference." However, in reality, a moment of self-focused thinking could accrue and develop into a detour from what God has for our lives. This is why it's especially important to keep our focus on Jesus and His truth when we face challenging circumstances.

Too often, Christians let twists and turns take them off the main road of their walk with the Lord. If we remember that He works all things together for our good, then we will not look for the nearest exit when the road gets bumpy. We will keep our eyes on Jesus, and this will keep us moving forward.

We must be vigilant to not let distractions take our attention off of Jesus. These distractions can be as simple as thoughts of how tired we feel, how far we are from our destination, or doubts about our past turns. While these thoughts may be common when we face hard times, we must do everything it takes to keep focused on Jesus. Over time, our perspective will change, and we will see how God was working in our lives all along, getting us right where we needed to be. What's needed in the middle of our journey is *faith*—the choice to trust God.

My encouragement to you is to never take your eyes off Jesus and His plans for you, especially in challenging times. Let these difficulties root you into the Lord even more than you were before. Make them an opportunity to keep the truth of God's love and goodness in front of you, so that the circumstance will strengthen your faith. Let God's nature be your guiding compass instead of your passing thoughts and feelings.

Perspective

Our perspectives are limited, and if we interpret circumstances through what we see rather than through the nature of God, we will be easily confused and discouraged. It's so easy to only look at what's right in front of us, especially when things are going wrong. However, what remains true? God works all things together for good, even if we can't see it yet!

A woven tapestry is a beautiful piece of artwork that takes an incredible amount of time and skill to produce. Each weave has to be extremely precise to create the final image. While the front of the fabric is intricate and beautiful, the backside of the fabric is another story. If you have ever seen the back of a tapestry, you would know that it often looks nothing like the front. It appears to be a mess of knots and lines of thread all mashed together. If you only ever saw the back of the tapestry but never flipped it over, you might conclude that the artist wasn't very skilled.

Many of us look at life with its daily struggles and challenges just as the person who looks at the back of the tapestry. Our lives sometimes look like a crazy, zig-zagging patternless collection of different experiences, all the while not realizing that from God's perspective, a masterpiece is being woven together one strand at a time. This is why it is so vital to only view our lives from the Lord's perspective. Only from a higher point of view can the true meaning and purpose of our day-to-day existence begin to emerge.

I believe many of us allow hopelessness to take root in our lives because we have not asked the Lord to reveal His perspective to us. If we knew what God is up to, what our purpose is, and what He is weaving together in us, we would never feel hopeless about where we are in life and what we are doing. We must not conclude God's nature from what we experience. We must, rather, redefine our experiences according to God's nature as revealed in His Word. We must allow His consistent goodness to create in us the expectation for good to come from even the worst circumstances. When we are rooted in this revelation of God's goodness, we cultivate expectant faith in our lives that attracts good things!

Eric's Story

Eric, one of the members of my leadership team, had dreamed his whole life about being a missionary and preaching the Gospel. Raised in a family that had been on and off the mission field, he grew up hearing stories from his parents and grandparents of preaching Jesus to the lost in the depths of the Amazon Jungle. He always responded by asking, "Why can't we go there now?!"

A few years ago, an opportunity opened up for him to move to Sri Lanka to educate and train new pastors in their understanding of the Gospel. Immediately, his heart jumped at the chance to go, but there was a problem; he had no money. For the next couple of years, he began reaching out to friends, family members, and churches, sharing his dream to go to Sri Lanka and asking for support. Little by little, money came in, but not anywhere near enough to reach the amount he needed.

Some time later, Eric received tragic news. His grandfather, who was a man of deep faith and a rock to his entire family, had a series of strokes. His family held onto the Word and its promises of healing, hoping to see him fully recover. After a long fight, his grandfather passed away. This was a difficult season for Eric, as he and his grandfather were very close. Saddened by their loss, Eric's family began making plans to hold a memorial service. Eric planned to use his own money for the flight home, but before he purchased the ticket, he got an email from someone he had never met before.

It was a friend of the family. He said that he had heard that Eric was living in California. Since he was only a few hours south, he offered to travel with Eric and cover all the trip's expenses. Eric agreed, and during the trip, connected well with this mysterious friend. They talked about life, ministry, the Word of God, and Eric's dream to go to Sri Lanka. The family friend seemed to probe at the topic of Sri Lanka, asking, "Why Sri Lanka? How long have you wanted to go there? What's holding you back? How much would you need to be fully funded?" Despite having never met each other before, the friend wanted to know as much as possible about Eric's dream.

Eric's time at home was as good as it could have been given the circumstances. His family came together in celebration of the life and legacy of his grandfather. When Eric returned to California, his heart was at peace, and he was ready to return to the normal pattern of life. However, God had other plans. During the trip, God had laid it on the mysterious friend's heart to fully fund Eric's nine-month trip to Sri Lanka. He reached out to our ministry, Grace Place, about the best way to give and to find out how much Eric would need. Within a week, Eric received a check for $12,000 from a person he had only met once in his life. God had done what He does best—He took even the aching pain of loss and orchestrated it for good.

Again, God is *not* the author of disaster, sickness, fear, destruction, or pain. Those things are the trademark signs of the works of the devil. First John 3:8 says, "...For this purpose the Son of God was manifested, that He might *destroy the works of the devil*" (emphasis added). You can be assured that it was not the will of God for Eric's grandfather to suffer a series of strokes, rapidly decline in health, and ultimately pass away. However, God's will was to orchestrate as much good as possible despite the situation and to bring about His plans in Eric's life. In Eric's own words, "God used the seed of my grandfather's life to produce something I was always made to do. The connections were no coincidence."

He is Glorified

All of us experience trial and heartache at some point, but how wonderful is it to know that Jesus is still the author of good in our lives no matter what we go through? This is why it is so vital to know and trust the nature of God. Not everything in life is good. However, God's promise to us is to make all things work together for good. Taking it a step further, God is *glorified* by working good in our lives. If something bad happens in our lives and God intervenes to make something good come from it, it reveals His nature and brings Him glory!

God promises to "work all things together for the good of... those who are the called according to His purpose" (Rom. 8:28). God has a bigger plan and purpose that involves all of us. When we face challenging circumstances, it can be tempting to make it all about us. We can be consumed with how life is affecting us and what we must do to overcome—but all these self-focused thoughts are simply more distractions that will take us off the main road if we are not attentive to move past them!

God took a hard circumstance in Eric's life and brought good from it—not just for Eric and the friend of the family, but for the nation of Sri Lanka as well! Just like individual moments are threads woven into one "tapestry" of life, each of our lives are individual threads woven into the tapestry of God's plan for all of humanity. God works all things together for good, creating a work of art from the noise and chaos that surrounds us. If we stay too focused on ourselves, we will miss out on the encouragement that comes from maintaining this perspective.

Look Up

We must keep our eyes on Jesus, or we will become too focused on the temporary circumstances we face. If we find ourselves discouraged by what we are currently facing, we can see it as an opportunity to be encouraged in the truth by refocusing on Jesus and what He has done for us. Otherwise, we will get fixated on ourselves and what we can do in our strength.

Jesus modeled a lifestyle of selfless love and was never focused on His own pain or glory. He knew that death on a cross was part of His Father's plan for the ultimate good and prosperity of all creation. When He faced the incredibly painful journey to the Cross and His ultimate criminal's death, He kept His eyes on the Father. He remembered how much He loved those He was dying for. We too must remain focused on God no matter what we face and allow His love for us to overflow into love for others. Then we will experience the supernatural grace of living selflessly.

I experience the grace that comes from selfless love regularly. When you are the head of a ministry that focuses on discipling young adults, late nights come as part of the responsibility. Over the past ten years, I have had countless late-night conversations, confrontations, come-to-Jesus moments, deliverances, etc. On more than one occasion, our entire leadership team has stayed up most of the night addressing issues and working through problems.

What I find interesting about these times is that when my focus is on others and their personal growth, I never feel tired the next day, no matter how late I go to bed. God's grace sustains me so that even if I get only a few hours of sleep, I still feel like I got a full night's rest. On the other hand, throughout my life, I have had many nights of staying up late to watch movies or hang out with people purely for fun. I wake up feeling tired instead of supernaturally energized. I have found that when my focus is on the Lord and loving those He loves, then He provides the strength to accomplish what needs to be accomplished. Grace comes in response to selfless love.

If we keep our eyes on Him and seek to glorify Him in all we do, we will experience His grace to walk through what's necessary. At the end of the day, our lives are not our own, and that is why we remain focused on Jesus despite the challenging circumstances we go through. There is a greater good that we are working toward, and God is so trustworthy that He will work things together for our good as well as the good of the Kingdom.

God does not desire to be our Friend and Provider on good days only. He not only blesses us when the sun is shining and the birds are singing and all is right with the world, but He's with us when we "walk through the valley of the shadow of death" (Psalm 23:4). God glorifies Himself by showing Himself strong in our weakness, our struggles, and our times of trouble. Jesus said that while things won't always be "easy," there is always hope in Him. "...In this world you will have trouble. But take heart! I have overcome the world" (John 16:33 NIV).

What situation in your life today do you need to see the goodness of God in? Where are the areas where life is not going as planned? Look for Jesus to glorify Himself there. In our weakness, He is strong. Psalm 27:13 says, "I would have lost heart, unless I had believed that I would see the goodness of the Lord in the land of the living." We must stand our ground on the fact that we *will* see His goodness on *this* side of eternity, and that His plans for us are good here and now.

> "Count it all joy when you fall into various trials, knowing that the testing of your faith produces patience. But let patience have its perfect work, that you may be perfect and complete, lacking nothing."
> — James 1:2-4

Part Three

ALL THINGS
ARE POSSIBLE

"Jesus said to him, 'If you can believe, all things are possible to him who believes.'"
— Mark 9:23

Chapter Seven

Limitless

There is no restriction, no limitation, and no cap on what we can do or accomplish. "All things are possible" is not just a cliché extracted from the Bible and nicely lettered on home decor—it's a reality that we must believe if we are to ever be the hands and feet of Christ on this planet. Jesus died, not just to forgive our sins, but to recreate us and set us free, to make us "free indeed" (see John 8:36). He died our death so that we could live His life and be filled with His Spirit, immune to the attacks of the devil.

Why does this limitless life feel like such a rare experience? Why do we face simple limitations such as sickness, fears, and the ever-elusive search for more time? It's not because all *reasonable* things are possible. Perhaps our minds have not been stretched to expect what we have not yet seen. To live a life without limits, we need limitless faith.

Jesus says in Mark 9:23 that "...all things are possible to him who believes." That's it—we must simply take Jesus at His word. When we rely on His promises, we will see the unlikely, improbable, and impossible happen every day. He says that those with faith the size of a mustard seed will be able to move mountains at a simple word (see Matt. 17:20). Many people interpret this figuratively, thinking that the "mountains" Jesus referred to were challenging days at work or your child having another meltdown. However, what if Jesus wanted us to expect truly impossible things to happen when we pray? What if we really could move mountains? According to early sources, this has actually happened before! Egyptian Christians in the early tenth century did just that.

In a time when Christians were persecuted in their places of gathering, a Fatimid caliph (prominent Muslim leader) challenged Christians to take their God at His word and demanded they move a mountain by prayer alone. He required them to raise the mountain from the ground. The Christians gathered and prayed, and the mountain rose above the ground three times in the very eyes of a shocked Muslim leader. The caliph allowed Christians to rebuild churches in the area after this miracle, and cave churches holding tens of thousands were built into the mountain.

This might sound ridiculous to you. It might make you skeptical. However, we have to take God at His word and believe that things on this scale are possible. We must allow our thinking to be stretched beyond "possibility." When we believe the impossible is probable, we will see natural limitations bow to the name of Jesus. What if we had a revelation of the faithfulness of God that motivated us to do the illogical?

Christ in Us

If you read this story and think, *I could never do that,* then you're in a good place! You're right—we can't do anything supernatural in and of ourselves. Without God, we are ordinary people with ordinary problems and ordinary solutions. It's God who does the impossible, but here is the good news: He has chosen to use us as His vessels!

Ephesians 3:20-21 (NIV) says, "Now to *Him* who is able to do immeasurably more than all we ask or imagine, according to His power that is at work within us, to Him be glory in the church and in Christ Jesus throughout all generations, for ever and ever!" (emphasis added). God does more than we could even imagine through His Spirit at work within us. It doesn't say, "Now unto *you* who is able." It says, "Now unto *Him* who is able." We can simply rely on Him when we find we do not have what it takes, and His grace (divine empowerment) will flow through our lives.

If we live according to our ability, we will be restricted according to our human limitations. We will "max out" when we get tired and after we've prayed our best prayers. However, if we live according to His ability, we will live according to His restrictions, and He has no restrictions! God is taking the limits off of our lives, pointing out that we can experience not only more than we have before, but more than we have even thought to imagine or ask for. He shatters our boxes by defining us by Christ's ability rather than our inability. God is taking the limits off of your life because He's not attaching you to anything other than Himself!

What are the most common things that keep people from accomplishing the call of God on their lives? Attitudes like discouragement, unbelief, and fear come to mind, as well as things like compromise, comparison, and past failures. What do all these things have in common? They all have to do with "me." If I don't follow God's plan for me, it's because of *my* inability, *my* insecurity, or *my* lack of preparation. All of our limits are focused on ourselves, and we feel limited when we focus on ourselves.

The more you look at yourself and say, "I can't do this" when you face challenges, then the more you're missing the answer. It's time to stop looking at yourself and your weaknesses and look at Jesus, who *is* the answer! Many people think that having confidence in Christ and what He can do through us is prideful. They spend time emphasizing their weaknesses in the name of humility. Sadly, these people do not understand that God's ultimate desire is for His children to rise up in the identity they have in Christ. They fail to enter into the fullness of what Jesus paid for, and they do not grow in Christ because they are weighed down by condemnation.

On the opposite extreme, others focus so much on their strengths that they step into pride. Some mistakenly take phrases like "I am a son!" or "I am royalty!" and use them to excuse behaviors that, in reality, do not align with who they are in Christ. Believing you are a son or daughter of God should naturally result in acting like one. Actions speak louder than words, and our behaviors confirm our beliefs.

It's true that we are God's royal sons and daughters. However, it's also true that, apart from Him, we are dead, rotten, and broken. Where's the balance between these truths? The balance is looking to Christ! We were once wicked, evil sinners, incapable of living in righteousness before Christ. Now, because of what *Christ* has done for us, we are royalty in His Kingdom with the ability to change the world. When we stay focused on Him, we will clearly see who we *are* despite who we once *were*! If we focus on ourselves, we will experience fear, pride, and condemnation. It's only in Christ that we have our victory. He who saved us is sustaining us!

Ephesians 3:20 says that His power *is* working in us, not that it *was*. The power of God is always working in your life! Salvation extends beyond the moment you said "yes" to Jesus. At that moment, His Spirit came into you, and He is now constantly working in and through your life. When you believe this, you will start to see it. Even in circumstances when everyone around you is discouraged, fixing your eyes on Jesus and declaring His reality will bring everyone back into alignment with the everlasting encouragement found only in the truth.

Because we are in Christ and Christ is in us, "...as He is, so are we in this world" (1 John 4:17). God never put limits on you. You put limits on yourself through your beliefs and self-reliance. So stop identifying with your feelings of inadequacy and start identifying with who you are in Christ. When we get our eyes off ourselves and onto Jesus, we will realize just how much is possible in our lives!

More Power Than We Know

God does even more through us than we could ever imagine ourselves capable of. Here is another powerful testimony told by one of my spiritual sons, Tyler, from one of our trips to South Africa.

Our guide knew of a witch doctor who lived in the village and led us to her house, hoping that we could set her and many others free. When we first arrived, the witch doctor was resistant and standoffish, not wanting anything to do with us and our God. In that moment, the Holy Spirit revealed to me that she had gotten into witchcraft to provide for and protect her family. I started to share with her what God was speaking to me and how the spirits she had invited in were actually hurting her and her family. I told her only one Spirit can help her, and His name is Jesus. She listened as I shared the Gospel with her, but she was still hesitant and opposed to what I was saying. We took time to talk with her more, get to know her, and share the perfect love of Jesus. As we shared, there was a moment when everything shifted, and she decided that she wanted to know this Jesus and give her life to Him forever! We prayed with her, and she surrendered her life to God.

She had a witch doctor's necklace and wristbands made out of beads and animal bones, specifically to draw power from spirits for witchcraft. Our guide explained that it was important to cut them off her wrists and take the necklace off her neck to bring total freedom and break the agreements she'd made with the enemy. She willingly agreed to remove them! I took a knife and cut the wristbands off her arms, and she removed the pieces around her neck. We led her through deliverance, and she told us how she felt the demons leaving through her eyes! There is no darkness that Jesus cannot conquer with His light. Our guide assured us she would continue to care for this lady. As we left that day, we knew we hadn't just saved one life but many who lived in the town.

This story amazes me because it shows that in the darkest places, God's light shines all the brighter, and He can always break through. Not only was this woman's life forever changed, but imagine what could happen to the lives of all the people who once came to her for "healing." Now they could receive true life from Jesus inside of her. All this was possible because Tyler walked in step with the Spirit of God, and the Spirit of God is not limited to what's naturally possible. It wasn't done through striving or struggling. The Gospel is the power of God unto salvation, and all of us have been equipped with this glorious Gospel! When we allow our lives to manifest the Good News of Christ, power is released.

No Limits

Read this statement out loud: The possibility, the reach, the limit, of anything or anyone is directly related to the source from which it comes! *Nothing can exceed the potential of its source.* This is why it is extremely important that we rely on Christ and not ourselves.

In Genesis 1, you'll find the well-known story of creation. I want to unpack this story to show you something that has set a premise for the way I live my life. In verse 11, God creates plant life, saying, "Let the earth bring forth grass, the herb that yields seed, and the fruit tree that yields fruit according to its kind." When He creates the stars, He says, "Let there be lights in the firmament of the heavens to divide the day from the night; and let them be for signs and seasons, and for days and years" (verse 14). When God creates the animals, He says, "Let the earth bring forth the living creature according to its kind: cattle and creeping thing and beast of the earth, each according to its kind..." (verse 24).

In each of these cases, God speaks to something He's already made to create something new. All of these created things had a source, and their sources were all other created things. What happens when you pull a plant out of the ground? It dies. What happens when a star falls from the sky? It dies. What happens when you take a cow and lock it inside a room for three months? It dies. Why? Because those things are no longer connected to their sources. They can only thrive when they are connected to their life source. Their possibility, reach, and limit are restricted by the environment they were born from.

In verse 26, God creates man. However, something is different this time: "Then God said, 'Let Us make man in Our image, according to Our likeness...'" God didn't speak to the ground or the sky when He made us—*He spoke to Himself!* Our possibility, our reach, our limit, is directly related to our Source: God, the Creator of the universe, who has no limits! Wherever we go, He is, and whatever He can do, we can do because He lives inside of us. We are not held back by the physical realm like the rest of creation because we weren't made in subjection to any other created thing. We have no limits!

Our union with Him is what makes all things possible in our lives. So are you faced with limitations today? Do you find yourself physically restricted or held back by fear? Look to Jesus, and you will realize that all things are possible!

Uniquely Qualified

On one of my mission trips to South Africa, one of the leaders on my team, Downing, was evangelizing at an outdoor shopping area. He approached a group of taxi drivers standing around waiting for customers and began sharing the Gospel with them. As he shared his personal testimony of experiencing God and overcoming guilt and shame in his life through the Gospel, one of the men said he wanted that as well. Downing led this man, Abongile, in a prayer to surrender his life to the Lord and then began praying for him to experience the baptism of the Holy Spirit. Abongile said he felt a ball of light rising in his chest as Downing prayed, and the higher it went, the lighter and happier he felt!

Downing explained the Holy Spirit to Abongile and how the same power that raised Jesus from the dead now also lives in him. At that moment, a lady, recognizing Downing as part of the missions team, approached him and asked if he could pray for her father who was waiting in the parking lot and was due for knee surgery the next day. Downing saw this as an opportunity for the taxi driver to see the power of Jesus alive in him. "Come on," Downing said to him, "I want you to see this for yourself."

He led the man over to Yonathan, another member of my team, and they went off together to pray for the lady's father. Yonathan showed Abongile, a man who had been saved for less than five minutes, how to pray, and then they prayed together for healing in the man's knees. Within moments, the lady's father was bending down on his knees, exclaiming he didn't even need his surgery anymore because he couldn't remember the last time his knees had felt that great!

God used a man who had just been saved minutes before to work a miracle in another man's body! What I love about this story is that it shows how God doesn't need you to be "mature" to move through you. He simply needs you to be available. Age doesn't matter in the spirit, only belief. I think many of us make up rules and regulations in our minds that we have to abide by in order to be "qualified" for God to use us. *If I read my Bible every day for a year, then God can use me. If I can get this sin problem under control, then God can do something with me. If I pray every day for two hours, God will be able to do something through me.* Reading your Bible, praying, and living a holy lifestyle are all great things. We should do them, but where in the Word do you see God telling us we have to do these things before we can move in power? These are man's conditions, not the Lord's.

This may sound offensive, but God isn't waiting for you to get your act together. He's waiting for you to believe in Him and take Him at His word (see John 6:29). Sadly, I see many in the Body of Christ today waiting for a point in the future when they will feel they are "good enough" for God to use them. If they persist in this way of thinking, these people could still be waiting ten, twenty, or thirty years from now, always finding another reason to disqualify themselves. However, the good news is that God does not rely on or even look at our perceived qualifications or disqualifications. In fact, God views our self-made righteousness, or our ability to be "right" without Him, as filthy rags (see Is. 64:6).

You see, we have been uniquely qualified by Jesus' death and resurrection. When He died, we died with Him. When He rose again, we rose with Him! "For [we] died, and [our lives are] hidden with Christ in God" (Col. 3:3). We now live as Christ on the earth! This is our source of empowerment for the supernatural. It is only when we look beyond what we can accomplish for God, what we can do in our own strength, and how perfect we can be, that we see the truth. Everything God required, Jesus has accomplished. The most important thing we need to do from this point on is trust in Him!

It's time for the Body of Christ to rise up in the knowledge of her identity, take Jesus at His word, and step out in faith. Often, we are too fixated on our own sense of worth, our own accomplishments, our past failures, or our up-and-down feelings and beliefs. However, if we focus on Jesus, remembering "[we] have been crucified with Christ; nevertheless [we] live, but Christ liveth in [us]," we will walk empowered by His Spirit (Gal. 2:20).

Unaccessed

Imagine for a moment that you have a bank account with one billion dollars. You have enough money to go out and buy whatever you want, whenever you want it, with no thought of lack. That would be nice, right? However, having all the money in the world would do you no good if you didn't know how to write a check or use a debit card. In other words, unless you know how to *access* what you have, having all the money in the world is of no value!

Similarly, we have been given every spiritual blessing in Jesus. The full weight and wealth of heaven is at our disposal—a Kingdom of possibility and power that we will never be able to exhaust. Yet many believers live their day-to-day lives in lack, not experiencing the reality of their rightful citizenship in Jesus' Kingdom. We have a responsibility to learn how to access what is freely ours by inheritance.

I would like to propose to you that the way to access your heavenly bank account is *not* found in self-righteousness, self-help, or trying to please God. It is by accepting that you are who He says you are: a son or daughter, fully loved and fully righteous, not by your own works, but because of the finished work of Jesus. We can do the "impossible" because Christ qualifies us by His work on the Cross! Because we are defined by Christ and not our own track records, we also have the same potential and ability as Christ. We are new creations, designed to do the same things Christ did.

Beyond All We Can Ask, Think, or Imagine

When I began to understand this revelation of the finished work of the Cross and that there was nothing I could do to further qualify or disqualify myself, I began to step out and take risks. I prayed for the sick, confident that God would move through me. Since then, I have seen incredible miracles that I never imagined I would see. Here's a testimony from a minister and personal friend of mine, Prophet William Undi, written in his own words:

I am William Undi, a pastor in South Africa. I travel the world as a prophet of God, ministering to nations.

On the first of March 2019, I suddenly became very sick to the point I couldn't walk, move my hands, eat, or see. I had a high temperature and struggled to breathe. My wife brought me to the doctor that day, and they tested me for 63 different diseases; all of them came back negative. I lost 44 pounds in the first five days. The doctors figured out that my blood was not flowing correctly, so they thought the condition had to do with the bacteria in my body. But they could not confirm a diagnosis, so for the next five days, they tried many different cures. They filled my body with steroids to the point that I lost the ability to talk, eat, or walk, and I lost my memory. The steroids damaged my liver so badly that I needed a liver transplant, and the doctor gave me only 10 days to live.

After spending 45 consecutive days in the hospital, the doctors released me to die at home. The day after I was released, Daniel Newton and his ministry team came to minister at my church. I was in no condition to go to the service, but Daniel texted me that whether or not I went, he still wanted to lay hands on me and pray. His faith for my healing gave me faith, so I was carried to the service and Daniel prayed for me. Right after praying, my wife said, 'Something just left you! You just gained your countenance back.' Later that day the whole Grace Place team prayed for me, and life began returning to my body. I could move my body again, and all pain left me. That same evening I was able to eat and drink again. Three days later I was completely healed as if nothing had happened!

I returned to the doctor for a check-up, and they saw my blood flow was normal, and I had a brand new liver. They had no medical explanation for my healing.

Three weeks after being healed, I was back to my regular routine of traveling and preaching. Now five months later I have been in six different countries and have had perfect health.

Hallelujah! This is one of the most incredible miracles I've seen. This was a situation that felt completely hopeless, and God turned it around in moments. I thank God that He does the impossible through us. We are not tied to doctors' reports or dire situations that seem like they could never turn around for the good. Praise God that He uses us as His vessels, and therefore all things are possible!

Walking as Jesus Walked

In Matthew 14, we find a story of the disciples taking a trip across the sea of Galilee without Jesus. The wind picked up and it began to rain. The water grew rough as they traveled deeper into the storm. Wind gusts pitched the little boat back and forth. After hours of fighting against the sudden onslaught, the disciples looked out across the rolling waves to see none other than Jesus. He was not in a boat. He was walking toward them on the water!

If the story ended there, it would be an amazing feat, but it gets even more interesting. Peter, seeing Jesus walking on the water, got a spark of revelation. "Lord, if it's you," he said, "tell me to come to you on the water." We can only speculate, but perhaps Peter knew that if it were truly Jesus walking on the water, that he would be able to do it too. Why? Because Jesus was never exclusive with His miracles. He always empowered His disciples. He never performed miracles to simply show off who He was; He performed miracles to *show us* what's possible when we believe.

Jesus did everything He did on earth as a man empowered by the Spirit. If He did all the miraculous things as God, His life is not one we should ever expect to replicate. We would remain limited and restricted. However, Jesus did everything as a man in order to show us what we can do with His Spirit in us. Jesus did miracles as a man who was walking in the power of the Spirit of God, and that is why we can do those same things too. If you have chosen Jesus Christ to be your Lord and Savior and you walk in the understanding of who you are in Him, the Spirit of God is within and upon you to do the same.

If Jesus was solely God and not man, there would be no ground for Peter to believe he could walk out to Jesus on the water. However, because Jesus was also a man, He was able to model what living in right relationship with God could look like. Peter was seeing a glimpse of the reality of Christ living in us, which is the hope of glory. When he stepped out of the boat and onto the water, he was stepping into the reality of the authority of God's Kingdom. We can do the same.

Jesus' life put the supernatural on display. It invites us into the impossible so that we too can transcend above the limitations of this world and walk in authority and power. When Jesus rose from the grave, He subjected all things beneath His feet, including the devil himself. Before He ascended, He commissioned us to reign with Him: "All authority has been given to Me in heaven and on earth. Go therefore and make disciples of all the nations..." (Matt. 28:18-19).

We are more supernatural than we think. Jesus "raised us up together, and made us sit together in the heavenly places in Christ Jesus" (Eph. 2:6). While we walk this planet, we also dwell in a higher realm together with Christ, and now we are the meeting point between heaven and earth. We live in two kingdoms: one we can see and one that we cannot. The one we cannot see is more real than the one we can. It is where our true citizenship lies.

Too often we limit ourselves based on what our natural minds can comprehend instead of by what the Lord says is possible. The apostle Paul once rebuked the Corinthian church for acting like "mere humans" (1 Cor. 3:3 NIV). We must realize that we are no longer mere humans, confined to our old sinful condition. "He has delivered us from the power of darkness and conveyed us into the kingdom of the Son of His love" (Col. 1:13). What is true of Christ is true of us, and what is not true of Christ is not true of us.

We define our limitations according to Scripture and the model of Jesus Christ, not according to what any man, situation, or past experience tells us. It is time we recognize our new lineage and position. We are only as limited as Jesus is, which is to say, not at all. In fact, Jesus Himself said we would do *greater things* than He did!

"Most assuredly, I say to you, he who believes in Me, the works that I do he will do also; and greater works than these he will do, because I go to My Father. And whatever you ask in My name, that I will do, that the Father may be glorified in the Son. If you ask anything in My name, I will do it" (John 14:12-14).

Imagine that! Read through all the gospels and look at all the amazing testimonies of what Jesus did. Food multiplication, shriveled limbs straightening, coins coming out of a fish's mouth, the dead being raised.... Jesus said we would do even greater things! Again, we are only as limited as the Holy Spirit is, and He is pure potential. What limitations have you put on your own life? What mountain is in your life that you're going around instead of seeing it move? It's time to take the limits off!

> *"The things which are impossible with men are*
> *possible with God."*
> — *Luke 18:27*

Chapter Eight

You're More Supernatural Than You Think

There is a common misconception believers have of the simple Gospel. We all understand that Jesus died for us, but not all of us know exactly what was accomplished when Jesus died and rose again. When Jesus died, we died, and when He rose to life, we rose to life with Him. As I've mentioned, Paul explains this well: " I am crucified with Christ: nevertheless I live; yet not I, but Christ liveth in me..." (Gal. 2:20). We are no longer the same people we were; we've been "born again" (see John 3). We have the Spirit of God Himself dwelling inside of us, "and the life which [we] now live in the flesh [we] live by faith in the Son of God, who loved [us] and gave Himself for [us]." We truly are in union with God.

Still, most Christians will agree with these statements without comprehending the true meaning of "union with God." I have seen a minister give an excellent illustration that helps explain the true nature of union. He takes two bottles of water and an ordinary glass. He holds the bottles up, pointing out that they are two completely distinct containers of water. As he pours both into the same glass, the water from both bottles become indistinguishable. In the same way, we are inseparable from the Holy Spirit in our union with Christ. He wasn't simply added to us. He's not like oil floating on top of water. He's become one with us in such a way that we will never be separated.

Christ died so that we could live. When He laid down His life for ours, a divine exchange took place. What was true of Jesus became true of us. In Christ, all restrictions become obsolete. We are limitless in Him because we are one with Him. For that reason, my two least favorite words in the English language are "I can't." Anytime I challenge someone to do something and they say, "I can't," I immediately respond with, "You can do all things!" While it's true that they cannot accomplish everything on their own, it's also an absolute lie that they are on their own to begin with. Only the devil could convince someone that they are incapable because Christ tells us over and over in His Word that we can do all things through Him! It is time to stop limiting the power of God in our lives and start realizing that if Jesus did it, we should too!

Jesus did not come to single-handedly show off the power of God on the earth. He came to establish a model for us to follow. Everything He did, He did as a man in right relationship with God to show us what we are capable of. The Word says that as Jesus is in the world, so are we (see 1 John 4:17). The incredible thing about that statement is that it says as He *is,* not as He *was.* To see who we are, we must see who Jesus is. In the four gospels, Jesus was God wrapped in human flesh revealing the nature and goodness of the Father. Now, however, Jesus *is* a life-giving spirit that dwells within us and reveals all things to us. The man Jesus, limited within a geographical place and time, did amazing things. Now that Jesus lives in us and is

no longer limited by time or geography, how much more can
He accomplish?

The Limitless Realm

There is a realm where there is no limitation, nothing to
hold us back. In this realm, we can do all things through Christ
who strengthens us. There is no sickness or fear. This is where
God speaks, heals, and does the impossible. It is a place where
there is no impossibility simply because limits do not exist
there. It transcends what we see with our eyes and feel with
our hands every day. What I am describing is the spirit realm,
God's dwelling place, and we have the ability to step into this
realm at any time. In order for us to tap into the dimension
of the unseen, all we need is faith. This moves us beyond the
place where we are limited by what we can taste, touch, and
see and opens us up to the place where we can partner with
the supernatural.

Peter accessed this realm when he took a step of faith
out of the boat and onto the waves. Instead of succumbing to
the logical conclusion that he would sink, he tapped into the
impossible and stood upon the waters. Whether he realized it
in the moment or not, he was partnering with the spirit realm.
He stepped into a position of authority we all have access to
through our relationship with God.

In John 15, Jesus teaches extensively on what it means to
"abide" in Him. He says, "I am the vine, you are the branches.
He who abides in Me, and I in him, bears much fruit; for
without Me you can do nothing" (verse 5). When we rest in
our union with Christ, we will be fruitful—in character, in the
supernatural, and in every area of life. This union with God is
the key to living a life of the impossible. Apart from Him, we can

do nothing, "but with God all things are possible" (Matt. 19:26). This is because God has no limits, and when we abide in Him, remembering we are one with the Spirit of God Himself, we are not tied to the limitations of the world.

Abiding in Christ is linked to abiding in the truth. John instructs his readers: "Therefore let that abide in you which you heard from the beginning. If what you heard from the beginning abides in you, you also will abide in the Son and in the Father" (1 John 2:24). When we hold fast to the truth, we will abide in God. This is why faith is so vital to the Christian life! This limitless life is the life of faith. Those who walk in the supernatural take Jesus at His word no matter what they face in their day-to-day life.

Faith Righteousness

Paul contrasts life by the Spirit with life under the law. In Romans chapter 8, he paints a powerful picture of the difference between a law-based mentality and a faith-based mentality—one that lives above man's restrictions. He explains that if we live self-righteously, we limit ourselves to what we are capable of. "Those who live according to the flesh set their minds on the things of the flesh, but those who live according to the Spirit, the things of the Spirit" (verse 5). Setting the mind on the flesh is to focus on man's strength and ability, or lack thereof. It is to fixate on this realm with its limitations, our past, and our failures. A mind set on the flesh is focused on sin and therefore wired to sin again and again: "for to be carnally minded is death (verse 6)."

However, if we depend on Jesus for our righteousness and stop working to earn it on our own, we are no longer limited to our own ability. Verse 6 continues to say, "to be spiritually minded is life and peace." We experience life and peace by focusing on Jesus, the reality of what He has done, and who we are in Him! Being in Christ frees us to live without limits, and we access that potential when we believe the truth!

What's the best part about this? Not only are you in the Spirit, but the Spirit is in you! We who are in Christ do not have to try to access the Spirit. Paul writes, "He who is joined to the Lord is one spirit with Him" (1 Cor. 6:17). We are one with the Spirit of God! In order to cooperate with the Spirit, we only need to yield to Christ in us. We do not have to pray extra long prayers for people to be healed. We do not have to *try* to be patient or gentle with people when they frustrate us. We do not have to struggle to forgive our neighbor. We must simply abide in Christ, and we will bear much fruit!

Faith Comes by Hearing the Word

Faith will spring up in our hearts when we meditate on Christ in us. We do not have faith in ourselves, but in "Christ in [us], the hope of glory" (Col. 1:27). He is our source of empowerment. We live by faith in Him because we have died and He lives in us. "[We] have been crucified with Christ; nevertheless [we] live, but Christ liveth in [us]: and the life which [we] now live in the flesh [we] live by the faith of the Son of God, who loved [us] and gave himself for [us]" (Gal. 2:20).

People often interpret these verses through a lens of condemnation, thinking, *I haven't received my breakthrough because I haven't believed enough. If only I had enough faith to receive what God wants to do in my life.* However, it's time for us to silence the voice of accusation once and for all, or else we won't receive the opportunity Jesus extends to us through His words. Our faith is in Christ because it's through Him that we can do all things. Faith actually comes from Jesus as a gift, not because we stir it up within ourselves.

Jesus speaks and life springs forth. Isaiah 55:11 says, "So shall My word be that goes forth from My mouth; it shall not return to Me void, but it shall accomplish what I please, and it shall prosper in the thing for which I sent it." His Word itself contains the power to accomplish what it was sent for. We do not have to strive to see it! Romans 10:17 shows us the fruit of receiving the Word of God: "So then faith comes by hearing, and hearing by the word of God." Faith is as simple as allowing the Word of God into our hearts. It's taking Jesus at His word and letting it spring up faith in our lives. When we do this, we will step out, not because we are motivated by pressure or the fear of condemnation, but because the Word itself will produce faith in our hearts to do what we never could before.

Paul makes it very clear that salvation does not come through works, and he reiterates this in almost every letter he writes. This was his core message: Salvation is not dependent on man's behavior but is available to all who will receive Jesus by faith. And this faith is not even of ourselves! We receive "by grace... through faith, and that not of [ourselves]; it is the gift of God, not of works, lest anyone should boast" (Eph. 2:8-9). If this great feat of salvation came by grace through faith, why would any aspect of the Christian life come by our own works? While it is true that "faith without works is dead" (James 2:26) and that we know we have faith by the works that manifest as a natural result, we must not put works ahead of faith.

Emphasizing works apart from union with Christ is actually separating faith from works, and "whatever is not from faith is sin" (Rom. 14:23). Working on our own is simply self-righteousness, which is "like filthy rags" to God (see Is. 64:6). In reality, this "works" mentality is not what will ensure our success as Christians, but it's what will limit us to our own potential and incapability. If we try to achieve faith rather than receive faith, we will be frustrated and condemned in our minds.

We must look "unto Jesus, the author and finisher of our faith" (Heb. 12:2). Faith begins and ends with the Alpha and Omega. He does not expect us to move from a place of faith to a place of works. "The righteousness of God is revealed from faith to faith," (Rom. 1:17) not from "faith to works." It says, "'The just shall live by faith,'" not by works. When we stay focused on Him, we will not be distracted by the "works" mentality. Jesus causes faith to come into our hearts by His living Word. It comes from Him.

Hebrews 11:1 says, "Now faith is the substance of things hoped for, the evidence of things not seen." Just because something isn't seen doesn't mean it does not exist. This is the key to faith: that we are eagerly expecting something there may be no visible evidence for. It's not about seeing, but believing. We must be childlike! This comes down to trusting the Lord. Faith springs up in our hearts when we rely on the Lord, trusting that He is able to come through for us just as His Word says.

Five Loaves and a Bag of Chips

On one South Africa trip, we sent a team out to spend the day playing with kids living in an orphanage in a very impoverished part of town. For hours they ran and laughed, carried kids on their shoulders, and played games with them. When lunchtime came around, a small room was opened where the team could debrief and eat the lunches they had brought. They hadn't been sitting long when one of the kids walking by the door peeped in, saw them eating, and shouted, "They have chips!"

Suddenly the small room was crammed with kids asking to share their food. The team of four knew they didn't have anywhere near enough food to feed all of the children. However, they combined what was left to see what they could give away. Together, they had two sandwiches, two small bags of chips, two chocolate bars, and two bananas. What happened next was amazing....

They broke the sandwiches in half and started giving pieces away to the hungry, reaching hands. They gave out countless handfuls of chips, a few apples, and at least six bananas. Finally, after all the kids had eaten as much as they wanted, the team took a tally of how many kids they managed to feed with such small provisions, and then it hit them: What they just did was impossible. If you only have two bananas, you can't give six children bananas. If you only have two sandwiches, you can't expect to feed a room full of children! However, that's exactly what they did. The food multiplied!

What I love most about this testimony is that none of them in the moment were thinking, "Hey, let's try to multiply food." Just like the boy who had five small barley loaves and two fish that fed 5,000, the team simply offered to Jesus what they had. Often we are most likely to see God move when we are not trying to make something happen but simply being who God called us to be. God loves little children, He satisfies the hungry, and He loves to surprise us with His goodness.

As I said early on, our nature is no longer merely human. We are now co-heirs and co-laborers with Christ. His Spirit dwells inside the heart of every person who believes in Him. We can therefore count on what is true about Jesus being true about us. We truly are more supernatural than we think!

Grapefruit Tumor

In one service in South Africa, we had a prayer line at the end of the service. As we were praying, a lady with a tumor on her stomach, the size of a grapefruit, walked by one of the members of my team in the fire tunnel.

Having never seen a healing before and not exactly knowing what to do, one student laid his hand on the tumor as the woman walked by to receive prayer. Before he could even say anything, he felt the tumor under his hand shrink down to nothing. He was completely shocked! I'll never forget his reaction as he saw the power of God move through his own hands for the very first time. All he could say was "that blew my mind!" What a testament to the unlimited power of God!

When you are in right relationship with God (this doesn't mean perfection; it means an open and honest heart before Him) and walking in His grace, nothing is impossible! Often, we limit ourselves based on what society and science deem "normal," but what is normal for man is abnormal for God. We should not water down the Gospel to meet our current level of belief or experience, but instead, let our experience transcend according to the truth of the Word. Jesus lives inside us now. We are destined to live as Christ did.

Did you know that, in Acts 5, God was moving so powerfully through Peter that people brought out their sick and laid them in the streets in hopes that Peter's shadow would touch them and heal them? Some might write that off as superstitious, but people don't go through the trouble of dragging others into the streets without an actual testimony of this happening. Let's not forget that this is the same man who denied Jesus three times!

Did you know that in Acts 19, handkerchiefs and aprons used by Paul would be brought to the sick? People were healed and delivered simply by touching items Paul used. It says that God worked *unusual* miracles through the hands of Paul. This is the same Paul who started as the super-Pharisee. He went from town to town persecuting the Church and witnessing many Christians being stoned to death. God can use whoever He wants, including you!

It's time we stop limiting God by deciding who He can and cannot use and let Him be free to move however He wants! It's time that we as the Church start being known for the unusual things that happen around us. What glory would it bring to God if people knew that all they had to do was step under our shadows to be healed? Or if someone was delivered by touching a shirt we wore? Or if a person who was once a racist, or murderer, or villain suddenly became a passionate lover of Jesus?

> *"I can do all things through Christ who strengthens me."*
> *— Philippians 4:13*

Chapter Nine

What is Your Limitation?

Luke 8 illustrates the well-known story of the woman with the issue of blood. This woman had dealt with a flow of blood for twelve years. She had spent all her money on trying to become well, and nothing had worked. In a final act of desperation, she fought through a crowd that surrounded Jesus to reach out and touch the hem of His garment.

A parallel portion of Scripture records that she said within herself, "If only I may touch His garment, I shall be made well" (Matt. 9:21). Obviously, this is a woman of great faith. She believed that all she had to do was reach out and touch the corner of Jesus' robe and she would be healed. And amazingly, she was! As soon as she touched the robe, Jesus felt power flow out from Him, and He knew someone had touched Him.

Many sermons have been preached and songs have been sung on this passage of Scripture exhorting us to simply "touch the hem of His garment," encouraging us to have faith like this woman. However, I would like to explore a different angle of this story. When Jesus asks who touched Him, the woman speaks up. He tells her, "Daughter, be of good cheer; your faith has made you well. Go in peace" (Luke 8:48). *Your* faith has made you well. *Your* faith.

What was the woman's faith in? It was in Jesus, but more specifically, it was in her ability to touch Him. "If only *I may touch his garment*, I shall be made well." For whatever reason, the woman had limited her faith to this very specific scenario playing out. Incredibly, she was healed and sent away in peace. However, notice the limitation she had placed on her faith. Jesus could have healed her in an infinite number of ways. However, she had limited herself to receiving from Him in only one very specific way. What if she hadn't limited her miracle to the action of touching Jesus' garment? Could she have been healed without pressing forward to touch Him?

Do you have a "hem of the garment" in your life? Is there a scenario or place in your life where you have been waiting for God to move but have limited your scope of how He can do it? It's time to take the limits off!

Let's contrast this with a story found in Matthew 8. Jesus had entered Capernaum when a Roman soldier came to Him, asking for healing on behalf of his paralyzed servant. Jesus offered to come with him, but the centurion refused. His response left Jesus in awe. He said, "Lord, I am not worthy that You should come under my roof. But only speak a word, and my servant will be healed. For I also am a man under authority, having soldiers under me. And I say to this one, 'Go,' and he goes; and to another, 'Come,' and he comes; and to my servant, 'Do this,' and he does it" (verse 8-9).

It says that Jesus *marveled* at the man's faith (Matt. 8:10). How amazing would it be to have faith that leaves Jesus speechless? The centurion understood authority. Understanding that Jesus could speak a word and it be carried out in the same way that the centurion spoke to his subordinates, he tapped into a deep level of faith. He did not limit Jesus' power or ability to travel all the way to his home to accomplish God's will. The word alone was enough.

The woman with the issue of blood said, "If I can touch his robe," but the centurion said, "If Jesus only speaks the word." Who had the more limited view of the power of Jesus? Both believed He was a miracle worker and a healer. Both people believed Jesus was more than able to meet their needs, but one had applied what they knew of authority, allowing it to strengthen his faith. One of these two had unknowingly put Jesus in a box, while the other had not.

Healed by the Word

I love being part of what God is doing and getting the opportunity to encourage churches to step more fully into what God is calling them to. During my ministry trips, I always make time in my meetings to pray for those who need miracles in their bodies. I have seen many people healed of chronic pains, terminal diseases, mobility problems, deafness, blindness, and many other conditions. I don't have to hope that God will show up when I lay hands on someone because the Word says, "They will lay hands on the sick, and they will recover" (Mark 16:18)!

However, a few years ago, the Lord challenged me on how I minister. I was in a season where the Lord was teaching me about the power of the Word of God. John 1 says, "In the beginning was the Word, and the Word was with God, and the Word was God," and "All things were made through Him (the Word), and without Him nothing was made that was made" (verses 1 and 3). In the beginning, God *spoke* and the world was established (see Gen. 1). There is power in the Word!

The Lord challenged me that when I speak using the Word, declaring the truth of the Gospel, power is released just like it is released when I lay hands on a person. It's like the story of the centurion. He recognized that Jesus could say "go" and the angels would "go" on His command. Following Jesus' example, we can speak the Word and see heaven move. Jesus Himself said, "Whatever you ask in My name, *that I will do*, that the Father may be glorified in the Son" (John 14:13).

Now every time I minister, before I ever lay hands or pray for anyone to be healed, I always give room for people to respond to the power of the Word. The Word itself carries the ability to restore, transform, and reconcile. I have seen many people healed simply by stepping out in faith after the Word has been preached. I ask them to test their bodies, move a little, and try to do something they couldn't before. Every single time, miracles happen. The best part is that these people aren't getting healed by me or a member of my team touching them but are healed just by putting faith in the power of His Word!

Sometimes people are offended because they are so used to the "normal" church services where they come forward to receive prayer for healing. Just like the woman with the issue of blood, many are thinking, *If only the man of God can lay hands on me and pray for my healing, then I will be healed.* When I ask them to test their bodies, they are hesitant, because no one has touched them, no one has even said a prayer yet. But what I want them to see is that just by the Word of God being spoken, the power to heal is present. I want them to raise their expectations and take their limits off. God is able to (and He *wants* to) heal! There's no formula or series of events that need to take place for His power to manifest. Where are we putting our faith? In the minister, a prayer, or a physical act? Or in the Word of God?

I ministered at a service in South Africa where one woman was missing a kneecap. She received a creative miracle just by responding to the Word. She left with a brand new kneecap in her leg! God worked a miracle in her body simply through her trusting the power of the Word. In another meeting, one young man testified that his sense of smell returned to him! If we can think or imagine it, God can go beyond it (see Eph. 3:20)!

No Limits

Most of us live our day-to-day lives surrounded by limitations. We live in carefully measured spaces, knowing fairly accurately what we are capable and incapable of doing. Conventional wisdom tells us to "know our limits" and not to push them too hard. As children, we dream of doing impossible things and changing the world, but by the time we are adults, most of us take on a more limited view of life. Like the woman with the issue of blood, we can all too easily become trapped in a set of self-imposed restrictions, limiting our scope of influence to what we can touch, see, and feel. However, often what we perceive as reality and what is true are very different things.

For example, before the summer of 1954, running a mile in under four minutes had never been done. Since at least 1886, it had been a goal that many runners tried to reach, and yet no one had. Eventually, this was deemed physically impossible, and some even went so far as to say the attempt could be fatal. Medical science said that the human body just wasn't made for that kind of exertion. From 1945-1954, the record mile time of 4:01.8 had remained unchallenged. Then came Roger Bannister.

In 1952, Bannister had competed for England in the Helsinki Olympic Games and had failed to medal at all. Coming home to harsh criticism, he resolved to do better. However, he did not just want to win a medal. He wanted to do what no one thought possible. He put himself into a rigorous training program, pushing his body harder than ever before. In the summer of 1954, he did what no man thought could be done. Finishing a mile run with a time of 3:59.4, he became the first man to complete a mile in less than four minutes.

What is interesting about the story of Roger Bannister is that his world record hardly lasted through the summer of 1954. In fact, since Roger Bannister's legendary victory, over 1,400 athletes have run a mile in under four minutes, and the current world record is 3:43.13! Why was it that, before Bannister, no one believed it was possible, and yet now, it is clearly attainable? What was it about Roger Bannister that was different? The answer is nothing. Nothing was physically different about Bannister than any athlete before him. The adjustment that was needed was not in training or skill, but in *mindset*.

The world had chosen to come into agreement with a narrative that said running a mile in less than four minutes was impossible, even dangerous. Many had tried, but no one had succeeded. Instead of continuing to try, growing better and closer every time, someone along the way suggested, "Why try?" Because no one had ever done it, common knowledge and conventional wisdom filled in the gap, creating a limitation.

As soon as one man broke through the ribbon in under four minutes, he broke through the limitation on humanity's mindset. He had accomplished the "impossible," and so it was no longer deemed "impossible." It became an achievable goal in the minds of other runners, and so they too accomplished a mile time of under four minutes. Once one man had done the impossible, the rest knew they could do it too. It's the same for us today! There's nothing too high, too wide, too deep, or too far away from the grasp of Jesus' power. If just one person believes it and grabs hold of it, the rest can follow in victorious pursuit.

Look to Him

If we remain satisfied with the progress we've made so far in our lives, we won't grow in expectation for the future. So often, when faced with a new challenge, we think back to the times we faced similar situations and how we handled them. We think, *Oh, last time I tried to climb a mountain, I had to stop halfway through,* or *Last time, I didn't get the promotion.* We meditate on the past and self-fulfill our negative prophecies! If we focus on failure and allow ourselves to get discouraged, we will not experience the abundant victory that is ours in Christ. We will define our lives by our ability and qualifications apart from Him. Instead, we must look to Him and rely on His grace (empowerment).

What we experience is closely linked to what we expect. We don't always get what we deserve, but we almost always get what we expect. We must discipline ourselves to see our circumstances through the lens of the Kingdom and Christ's power working in us. We must have faith that He can do more than is logical or likely according to worldly wisdom. When we train ourselves in this hopeful attitude, our expectations will begin to manifest.

If you can see it, you can have it. Your thoughts are the preview of your life's coming attractions. In any area you want to see growth, choose to *see* that growth now. Envision where you want to be and meditate on what it will look like. This faith in action will increase your anticipation and position you to receive the very breakthrough you're wanting.

Our experience shouldn't dictate the Word of God. For that reason, we also shouldn't let our current state of being limit our belief in our potential. What if the most limiting factor in our lives was the *belief* that we are limited? What would happen if we took the limits off our belief and trusted Jesus to do the impossible in and through us?

What Are You Expecting?

When praying for blind men to see, Jesus tells them, "It shall be done to you according to your faith" (Matt. 9:29 NASB), and their eyes opened. In the Passion Translation, it says, "You will have what your faith expects!" Jesus implies that the faith of these men was the access point to experiencing the miraculous. As He prays for healing, Jesus is also showing people the doorway to the impossible: their faith.

On my trips to South Africa, we see incredible healings as we walk the streets and go house-to-house through neighborhoods. However, in the Western world, these miracles are more rare. Why is this? Is it because it is easier to heal the sick in Africa? I believe it is because the spirit realm has become very familiar to the South African people. The overly-intellectual perspective of Western culture has not corrupted their healthy understanding that there are always spiritual forces at work. Angels, demons, miraculous healings, and other "impossibilities" are common in their culture. Modern medicines that we utilize here in the developed world are far less available and much more expensive in other places, so they turn to witch doctors or pastors when they need healing.

In Africa, the need for the supernatural is much more real. However, I do not believe that God is more active in the poor places of the world than in First World countries. I believe we would see the same here in the United States and around the globe if we became more accustomed to the reality that what God does in one place, He wants to do everywhere else.

What's Available?

Too many Christians today are living without awareness of what is accessible to them. They do not understand who they are in Christ, so they are limited to the same potential of every other person on the planet. However, if they knew what Jesus accomplished for them and that they must only access it by faith, then they would experience the impossible.

Believing the Gospel is as simple as breathing. We are surrounded by oxygen—an unlimited supply of it! But if our beliefs about oxygen were the same as our beliefs about God's grace, many of us would be holding our breath right now! We are surrounded by an unending, completely free supply of breathable, life-giving air. All we have to do... is *breathe*. If we felt oxygen was running out or that we weren't worthy of the free gift of air, we would live in fear and eventually die due to our own self-condemnation. How foolish would that be? All we have to do is open our mouths and inhale the air that's all around us!

I heard Pastor Bill Johnson from Redding, CA tell this story once that stuck with me:

Imagine there was a man who went on a cruise. He had saved up his money to take his whole family, and they were very excited! They had just enough money for the basic cruise with no upgrades, so they packed their own food. Every day during the lunch hour, they would walk past the busy buffets and sit as a family on the deck, happy to simply enjoy their vacation together.

It wasn't until the last day of the cruise that someone asked them why they were eating packed lunches from home. A bit embarrassed, the man explained that they had just enough money to pay for the baseline cruise with no upgrades or extra meals and activities. The man told them: "Don't you know? The food is complementary!" I can just imagine the disappointment of the family as they realized they had settled for less than what had already been paid for.

I can only imagine what Jesus must feel when we do the same thing to Him. He's bought for us a life without restrictions. However, many Christians don't even know what is available for them, and they don't care to ask. Instead, they are growing weary as they work for what Jesus already gave them freely, or worse yet, they never even think of the inheritance that is rightfully theirs.

As soon as we take Jesus at His word, we can break out of these boxes of worldly thinking that we've been raised in and become vehicles of the supernatural here and now. Jesus promised that we will do even greater things than He did, so why would we stay stuck, expecting to live a lesser life than He lived?

Break Them Off

What limitations have you put on your own life? What's the thing that's holding you back? Have you ever tried something and failed? How did you deal with it? How we deal with failure is far more important than the failure itself! If we take any failure to the Lord and ask for His grace (and forgiveness, if we've sinned), eventually we will succeed. If the Lord is calling us to something, we will always see breakthrough if we do not give up. However, if we let failure become our excuse rather than our teacher, we will eventually give up. We were never born to quit. This is a subject I'm very passionate about. We must develop the grit to say, "No matter how many times I mess up, quitting is not an option!" (For more on this topic, check out my book *The Lost Art of Perseverance*.)

There is only one person who has the power to set limitations over your life, and I am not referring to the Lord or the devil. That person is you! Has the enemy been using an inferior belief system to toy with your mind? God wants to renew your mind and set you free completely. Stretch your thinking far beyond where it's gone and start to dream for the impossible.

For the remainder of this chapter, I am going to share stories that are completely true but also completely impossible. These are the stories of men and women who walked with God and saw "unbelievable" miracles happen. I want these stories to challenge your assumptions of what is possible because, "With God, all things are possible." It's time we put the *"all"* back into *"all things are possible!"*

The Wolf of Gubbio

Saint Francis of Assisi was an Italian monk who lived from 1182 to 1226. He was a passionate follower of Jesus known for his connection to nature. In one of his most famous stories, Francis traveled to the town of Gubbio to preach the Gospel. When he arrived, he was surprised to discover the town was being terrorized by a wolf from the nearby forest. The wolf would frequently appear in the city, killing both animals and people. The townspeople were forced to shut themselves within the city walls in fear of the wolf.

Francis, having compassion on the people, left the city and ventured into the forest in search of the wolf. After traveling for some time, the wolf suddenly charged to attack him. When Francis saw the wolf charging at him, he made the sign of the Cross and said, "Brother wolf, come to me." The wolf immediately came and sat down at his feet. It looked up at Francis eagerly, ready to listen. Francis explained the terror he had been inflicting on the townspeople and commanded him to stop. He made a deal with the wolf that if the townspeople would protect it and feed it, it would not attack the city anymore or kill any of the people or animals. By Francis' request, the wolf held out its paw to accept the proposed pact.

From that point onward, the wolf lived among the residents of the town doing no harm. They lived together in peace and, after the wolf died, the townspeople constructed a statue of the wolf to commemorate the miracle that had been worked by Francis on their behalf.

Sailing on a Cloak

Francis of Paola, another well-known saint, needed to go from the mainland of Italy to the island of Sicily. The journey is a distance of about two miles over rough Mediterranean waters. Francis found a boat in one of the harbors and asked the captain if he would be willing to take him and his companion across.

The sailor replied gruffly, "If you pay, monk."

"For the sake of Christian charity, my brother," Francis said, "take us across to the island in your barque."

"Then I have no ship for you," the sailor replied as he sent them away, mocking them.

Francis, unwilling to give up on the journey, walked to the shore and prayed. Then, to the captain's shock, he stepped out onto the waves. He laid his cloak on top of the water, tied one end to his staff as a sail, and sailed across with his companion on top of the floating cloak. The captain repented of his selfishness and offered to ferry Francis across any time in the future.

A Newborn Speaks

Saint Anthony of Padua, a contemporary of Saint Francis of Assisi, was another monk that experienced great miracles. In his town of Padua, Italy, there was a man who dealt with extreme jealousy toward his wife. She had never been unfaithful to him, but no matter what she said or did, he was convinced she was unfaithful. When they had their first child, the man's obsession became so strong that he refused to recognize the baby as his own.

Unable to convince him of the truth on her own, the woman desperately turned to St. Anthony for help. Anthony counseled the man for hours, attempting to help him see the error in his thoughts and how absurd his jealousy was. Just when they were beginning to make progress, a nurse walked in with the infant. In a flash, all reason left the man, and he resumed attacking his wife's character and the child's legitimacy.

Anthony, determined to resolve the situation, turned to the newborn and said, "In the name of Jesus Christ, speak and tell who your father is!" The child pointed at the man and said in a much older child's voice, "There is my father!" The man, amazed by what he had just seen, broke down in tears, repented, and took the child into his arms.

Protecting the Innocent

Saint Anthony's elderly father lived far away in the capital of Portugal, Lisbon. One night a murder was committed on the street outside his home. The murderer, seeking to frame someone else, threw the victim's body over the wall into Anthony's father's garden. The authorities arrested him and, after a trial and imprisonment, sentenced him to death.

News reached Saint Anthony in Italy of his father's fate, and he quickly came to his aid. He sought to convince the judge of his father's innocence, but the judge would not be swayed in his sentence. The evidence pointed to his father's guilt, and his innocent father was about to be killed as punishment. In the courthouse, Anthony got everyone's attention. He asked the court to follow him out into the cemetery, where he led them to the grave of the victim. He ordered the grave to be exhumed, and once the coffin had been unearthed and opened, he commanded in a loud voice for the dead man to bear witness as to whether his father murdered him. The dead man sat up, raised one hand, and said, "This man is not my murderer."

The dead man laid back down and was reburied. Anthony's father was set free and released from all charges. The judge pressed Saint Anthony to ask the dead man who was his true murderer, but Anthony refused, saying, "I have come to save the innocent, not betray the guilty."

"Death, Come Out"

Smith Wigglesworth was a man of great faith. He lived in England in the late 1800s. He was a humble man with a deep passion for the Lord who witnessed many supernatural healings and miracles. One day he was called to the house of a woman with many tumors. He knew by looking at her condition she did not have long to live. Wigglesworth asked her, "Do you want to live?"

She could not speak but began to move her finger in answer. Before she could get her point across, however, she died. The woman's young daughter came to the bedside, and Wigglesworth was moved with compassion. He picked up the deceased woman and carried her across the room. Standing her against the wardrobe and holding her up, he shouted, "In the name of Jesus, death, come out!"

While still holding her up, she came back to life. When she could stand on her own two feet, Wigglesworth let her go and said, "In the name of Jesus, walk," and the woman walked back to bed.

Blight Cured

One day, Wigglesworth went to visit the farm of a close friend. Looking out at one particular field, he commented on how beautiful it was. His friend sighed and said, "It's not what it looks like. The whole field is ruined by blight." Wigglesworth was moved with compassion for the man and his situation. He lifted his head in prayer, stretching his hand out over the field. The whole field was cleansed of the blight, and the entire crop was saved. In fact, that season's crop ended up being the best the farmer had harvested from any of his fields.

A Life of "All Things"

The miracles you just read about are more than "cool stories." They are your inheritance. They are your portion. They are your calling. Should you copy and paste their stories into your life and mimic their actions? Not necessarily. You can do greater things, different things, things that make the world wonder who your God is. Your faith in Christ is full of possibilities. There are no limits to what you can create and no walls to withstand the miracles you can perform. You were designed to be a vessel for the God of *all things*.

Conclusion

"We get caught in our boxes, but when we pray outside of them, ask God, the impossible CAN be done."
— *Loren Cunningham*

When you put this book down and face the realities of everyday life, remember who you are. You are a co-creator, a miracle-worker, a holy priest, and most importantly, you are *His*. He has made all things new, not just today, but always. He has provided all things for you, not just once, but anytime you're in need. He is working all things together for your good, not just when you deserve it, but when you believe for it.

Fix your eyes on Christ. Abide in Him. When life tries to negotiate with you, offering you *some* things, don't settle. When *some* things feel new and *some* things work out well, don't stop. Keep going, keep believing, and keep receiving. You were never made for *some*. When the Father sent His only begotten Son, did He offer *some* of Him or *all* of Him? Jesus Christ gave everything He was for you, down to His very last breath. The Bible says He was *emptied* on your behalf. The fullness of everything He is, is reserved for you.

We are one with Christ. What is true about God is true about us, and what is not true about God is not true about us. I believe the day is quickly approaching when there will cease to be a difference between how we, the Body of Christ, perceive ourselves and how God sees us. Our lives should align with Scripture, and it is there that we find our true identity. We must understand who God has made us to be and live the life we were created to live—a life without limits.

All things have become new, all things work together for good, and all things are possible—these three phrases summarize the whole Gospel. He has redeemed our past, He is moving in our present, and our future destiny is to look just like Him! When we become fully convinced of these three truths, there will be nothing we cannot do!

I challenge you to take what you've read and allow it to change your view of God and His work in every area of your life. Dare to believe you will see the impossible happen in your life. Receive Christ's faith for it. It's not about the size of your faith, but who your faith is in. Jesus said, "...if you have faith as a mustard seed, you will say to this mountain, 'Move from here to there,' and it will move; and *nothing will be impossible for you*" (Matt. 17:20).

Take risks, dream big, step out in faith, and take God at His word. Don't allow the impossibilities that surround you to limit what God can do. He is truly unlimited and, as a child of God, so are you! So break down the walls that surround your mind, shatter the boxes that imprison your heart, and come alive to the immeasurable potential found only in Christ! Face your challenges with new grit, fresh assurance, and burning conviction. It is true and will never cease to be true that, with Him, ALL THINGS are possible!

About Grace Place

Grace Place Ministries is a discipleship community fueled by a passion to see God's people walk out their identity in Christ and establish His Kingdom upon the earth. We are committed to developing mature Christian leaders through one-on-one mentoring, building family through weekly gatherings, and providing leadership opportunities designed to facilitate connection and growth. We travel frequently to minister around the world and create resources to build up the Church in her righteous identity.

Vision

Mature sons and daughters
established in their identity in Christ,
spreading the Gospel of grace and truth.

Mission

Disciple young adults.
Minister around the world.
Resource the nations.

DISCIPLESHIP IS OUR MISSION; WILL YOU JOIN US?

Now, more than ever, the body of Christ needs to arise and shine. The world is searching for answers and is in need of an encounter with God's love and truth. Who will raise up a generation to bring answers our world is desperately seeking?

"For the earnest expectation of the creation eagerly waits for the revealing of the sons of God."
– Romans 8:19

Whether it is a young man or woman needing a mentor or an entire church seeking the resources to disciple their community, you can make an impact!

BECOME A PARTNER WITH GRACE PLACE MINISTRIES:

GO TO:

WWW.GRACEPLACEPARTNER.COM

Grace Place Ministries

Additional Resources

The Lost Art of Discipleship
God's Model for Transforming the World

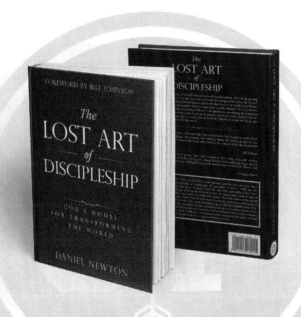

Discipleship is not a man-made idea. It is God's design for world transformation. *The Lost Art of Discipleship* is the uncovering of heaven's blueprints for remodeling the kingdoms of the earth into the Kingdom of our God. In his cornerstone book, Daniel Newton pulls from 20 years of experience in discipleship. As you read, prepare your heart to be ignited with the fires of revival that once swept the globe as in the days of the Early Church. It is time for the people of God to arise and shine for our light has come!

Available at www.GracePlaceMedia.com

@GracePlaceDiscipleship

ADDITIONAL RESOURCES

THE LOST ART OF DISCIPLESHIP
Workbook

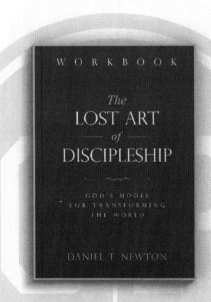

Enrich your understanding and increase your mastery of God's model for world transformation. This companion workbook to *The Lost Art of Discipleship* book is filled with exclusive content, in-depth exercises, and practical coaching to introduce a lifestyle of discipleship in your day-to-day walk. Whether you have been following the Lord for years or recently surrendered your life to Jesus, this manual breaks down the Great Commission and equips you for a life of fruitfulness!

Available at GracePlaceMedia.com

@GracePlaceDiscipleship

Additional Resources

The Lost Art of Discipleship
Online Course

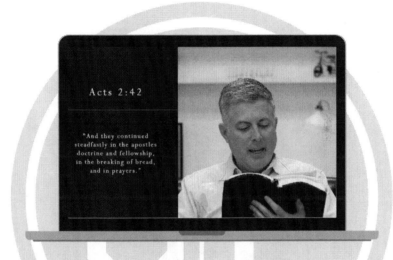

You can live the Great Commission. Every believer is called to embrace Jesus' final command: to make disciples... and this interactive online course is designed to take you even deeper into the rich content taught in *The Lost Art of Discipleship*.

Whether you are wanting to position yourself as a son or daughter, lead as a father or mother, or create a culture of discipleship, this course is for you! Rediscover the lost art with over five hours of video content, practical teaching, quizzes, and supernatural activations from Daniel Newton.

Available at GracePlaceMedia.com

@GracePlaceDiscipleship

ADDITIONAL RESOURCES

IMMEASURABLE
Reviewing the Goodness of God

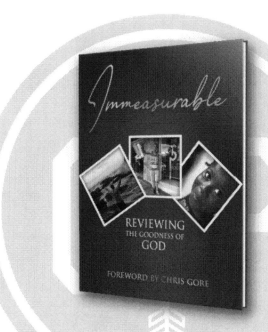

You are made in the image of the Miracle Worker, designed to manifest His glorious nature. *Immeasurable: Reviewing the Goodness of God* is a collection of 100 real-life stories of salvation, healing, deliverance, signs and wonders, reconciliation, and provision. Every miracle is a prophetic declaration of what God wants to do in, through, and for someone just like you.

ADDITIONAL RESOURCES

TRUTH IN TENSION
55 Days to
Living in Balance

NEVER GIVE UP
The Supernatural Power of
Christ-like Endurance

Other Titles

THE LOST ART OF PERSEVERANCE
Rediscover God's Perspective on Your Trials

Available at www.GracePlaceMedia.com

@GracePlaceDiscipleship

ADDITIONAL RESOURCES

GP MUSIC: BEGINNINGS

Everyone has a story. Most people don't realize that God doesn't just want to improve their story. He wants to rewrite it. Beginnings offers a fresh start, a new focus. This worship album invites you into the core anthems of grace and truth which have impacted us at Grace Place.

Our prayer is that this album helps you lay down your past mistakes, your present circumstances, and your future worries in order to lift both hands high in surrender to the One you were created to worship. We ask that you join us in a new beginning — an exciting start to a life filled with perseverance, focus, and surrender.

Available at GracePlaceMedia.com

@GracePlaceDiscipleship

KEEP US UPDATED

We would love to connect with you and hear about everything
God has done in your life while reading this book!
We also would love to hear how we can be praying for you.
Submit a testimony or prayer request by going to
GracePlaceRedding.com/mytestimony

STAY CONNECTED WITH GRACE PLACE

Are you interested in staying up to date with Grace Place Ministries
and receiving encouraging resources via email?

VISIT OUR WEBSITE:
GracePlaceRedding.com

SIGN UP FOR OUR NEWSLETTER AT:
GracePlaceRedding.com/newsletter

FOLLOW US ON SOCIAL MEDIA:
@GracePlaceDiscipleship

Made in the USA
Columbia, SC
29 October 2022

70176332R00091